PROVOKED IN VENICE

Wesleyan Poetry

Mark Rudman

PROVOKED
IN
VENICE

Wesleyan University Press

Published by University Press of New England

Hanover and London

Wesleyan University Press
University Press of New England, Hanover, NH 03755
© 1999 by Mark Rudman
All rights reserved
Printed in the United States of America

5 4 3 2 1

CIP data appear at the end of the book

Thanks are due the editors who were willing to devote space in their journals to the following sections of this book. Also note that some of the poems were published under provisional titles.

The Alembic: The "Real" *Revolt*
Arion: Against Odds Against, The Desert of Empire, In Your Own Time
The Denver Quarterly: The Assassins
Kenyon Review: Joan and Jean
New England Review: Revolt, "Study for Male Gaze"
Ploughshares: Tomahawk
The Progressive: Early Deliveries No One Receives
Sewanee Review: Provoked in Venice, as Provoked in Venice I, "Normalissimo;" Venice Less and Less, as Provoked in Venice IV
Triquarterly: Venice: The Return in Winter, Evening on the Zattere, Love at Last Sight, Tell Me Why, Midsummer Night in Venice
Verse: Stealth, as Provoked in Venice 7

Grateful acknowledgment is made to the John Simon Guggenheim Memorial Foundation and the National Endowment for the Arts for fellowships granting time to complete this book, and to The American Academy in Rome for providing space and human fellowship.

For Madelaine and Samuel

Comparing the post-World War II Italy they know [hundreds and thousands of Englishmen and Americans who have made an Italian journey of their own] with the pre-French Revolution Italy which Goethe saw . . . I am amazed at their similarity. Is there any other country in Europe where the character of the people seems to have been so little affected by political and technological change?

W. H. AUDEN on Goethe's *Italian Journey*

FAL: . . . and that sprightly Scot of Scots, Douglas, that runs a horseback up a hill perpendicular—

PRINCE: He that rides at high speed and with his pistol kills a sparrow flying.

FAL: You have hit it.

PRINCE: So did he never the sparrow.

WILLIAM SHAKESPEARE
Henry the Fourth, Part 1. Act II, Sc. IV

Contents

I REVOLT

"Normalissimo"   3
Revolt   8
Against Odds Against   19
The "Real" *Revolt*   22
Brecht Looks at Xeriscaping With a Thought About Shelley   35
The Assassins   37
A Winter Night in the City of God   43

II THE DESERT OF EMPIRE

Provoked in Venice   59
Evening on the Zattere   65
From What Angle   69
The Desert of Empire   73
"Not Normalissimo"   77
Venice Less and Less   88
Tomahawk   98
Across a Crowded Room   102
Phaeton's Dream: Driving Lessons in the Desert   115

III DYING AND FLARING

Joan and Jean   129
Stealth   152
The Last Night of a First Trip to Venice   158
Without a Care in the World   160
Midsummer Night in Venice   163

Tell Me Why   164
Early Deliveries No One Receives   168

IV   THE RETURN

Venice: The Return in Winter I   173
Venice: The Return in Winter II   176
In Your Own Time   197

Notes   201

I

❧

REVOLT

"NORMALISSIMO"

I

Archival Material

Skylines—the vertical passion parallel to our own.
The slow barges on East River and Hudson, circling.
Human beings: vertical creatures in a horizontal world,
set naturally against nature, against architecture:
this eye-soring puzzle of roofs, straight up and down;
lines broken only by water towers
poised like spaceships to lift off in the mist.
But in Rome the sprawl grows endlessly on all
sides of the Tiber, breaks down, honors
the jaggedness of ruins, walls the impatient
prophets once hopped eagerly to glimpse
a wry indeterminate future.
It grows harder by the hour to have a moment alone
and free from technos encroaching as this third
millennium approaches, but we find time,
before pouring onto the parasol-studded black sand
at Ostia-by-the-Sea
to have a few long gulps of warm peach tea.

I'm glad that you had the decency to make some mention
that in spite of the traffic, and your American friend hysterical

(and stalked by her husband on the cell-phone she kept on her
    person at all times:

why should she and their two sons gallivant while he lay
dying . . . impatiently . . . without enough oxygen getting to his brain
to keep him sane,

which she assures me he had been
when they tied the knot)

3

about running out of gas and arriving at another closed ruin,
you still got a few moments to yourself at the old port itself,
which is its own . . . revenge.

2

Ostia

A minute of silence in the deserted amphitheater.
Antique instruments compel the emptiness,
like the ram's horn blown on Rosh Hashanah.
And the ones who scurry through the site
as the gates are closing pause only
to shoot each other on the absent stage.
No matter. I was destined to leave
soon anyway because three young boys
are dying for a swim promised in exchange
for enduring (*yet another?*) ruin.
And what about the fun they are having
saving this old port from the barbarians.
Being always surrounded by danger
becomes another way of being.

3

"Normalissimo"

My father dragged me to Florida as a child
where I was appalled to see miles
of bodies, slathered with Coppertone,
spread out on chaise lounges.

There seemed no point: why was this
superior to staying in my room
and watching television.

Or go the way of that which history
claims in the instant of its vanishing

of that which was once known
as history, and not a meager stream
of candidates for obsolescence; like
out of print classics; and dreams.

This is the very image of our time:
someone answering a question as if
it were an accusation. No wonder

my American friend who resides in
Rome couldn't let go of the way the girl's
mother—in reply to my question—

said that the white, shell-shaped "chips"
her daughter crunched dragging
the crackling cellophane bag

over Ostia's black sand

were "*normalissimo*," wielding the word
with an emphasis that made us all

angry, and suspicious, because her tone
was so damn condescending.

A dash to the snack bar at closing time.
Forefingers tapping digital watches.
Shaking heads grunting
"chuiso, chuiso."

But it would take more than a
grizzled gruffness on automatic pilot
to keep us, manic and determined,
from checking out *what was in those chips.*

Miranda challenged the Italians in fluent
Italian with "what'stheproblemthesechildren
havetoeatorthey'lllevitateandyoucanthen
peelthemoffthewalls."

Of real potatoes—no sign
amidst the arcane, polysyllabic list
of artificial substances to rival
Homer's catalogue of ships.

The word—and the way she said it—
preyed on our minds,
like an ominous sign, or an emblem
of a value system out of science

fiction, legitimizing this obscene
blind, sweeping "normalissimo."

♣

She was in this a true descendant of Mussolini, who worked like the devil to put some order in the chaos that was Rome.

"We can't change our nature but we can change the way things are done."

You mean dub every foreign film so that people don't get any wrong ideas.

Hey little devil who do you think created your beloved Cinecittà, *where so many of the films you're so crazy about were made?*

I'm not sure about that.

That's where the Italian films are made.

No kidding. (Pause.) I'm not sure that the ones made in Cinecittà are the ones I've taken to heart, but there are probably some.

What about that utterly boring drivel you once convinced me to see in Colorado, Contempt, *which you've been obsessed with for reasons I'll never never never understand since you first saw it at an impressionable age one Saturday at some nuthouse, I mean "art theater," tucked away in some back alley in Phoenix.*

Can we come back to that? I was beginning to move in another direction when you broke in.

You mean can I wait? Why not, what else is there to do in heaven, other than gamble with the gods who stack the odds against the dead even more than the casinos of earth do against the living?

I never thought about it at the time
(in Miami every Christmas break

due to my father's mania for being "burned black"),
the issue of a Jewish constituency,

or of how this form of luxury,
equal sign drawn between

darkening skin and good health—
might be revenge for wounds

incurred during the war

most of these people were too old to have fought in—

but the right age to note "the horror"—

There was still something mysterious
        about this clannishness, this clinging to
            Coppertone and *Delicatessen*
        like religion.

REVOLT

I

— That was normalissimo *too.*

That woman lived her life to possess this cabana at Ostia-By-The-Sea,

(like the screenwriter's wife at the start of that long out of print Moravia novel,

what the hell is the title?

A Ghost at Noon.

who is consumed by the desire
for a bigger and better apartment
in a (higher?) high rise)

and for her daughter to have the privilege to munch the latest in "snack" foods—

which for all you know has been approved for space flights . . .

the chemicals may be nutritional improvements over so called "real" ingredients, like that killer, salt, and that carbo-bomb, potato . . .

The cheesiest video joints carry a dubbed version of *Contempt,* the film Jean Luc Godard improvised around Moravia's themes.

CONTEMPT OR *LE MEPRIS*
Director: Jean-Luc Godard
Cast:
Brigitte Bardot as Camille, a secretary
Fritz Lang as Fritz Lang
Jack Palance as Jerry Prokosch, an American producer
Michel Piccoli as Paul, novelist and screenwriter

8

And the coital "B.B" (Brigitte Bardot) on the box is not the "B.B." (Bertholt Brecht) quoted by Fritz Lang in the film.

I think that both Brecht and Pavese would have liked the cutting of causal links, psychologizing, explanations, the . . .

hint of omniscience despite the singular point-of-view?

. . . in Godard's, focused yet sumptuous, disorienting yet powerful, "tragedy in long shot" . . . .

Sometimes we don't do so badly, you and I. And then you'll turn against me, without warning, like a storm breaking in a cloudless sky.

A sky that's cloudless to the eye.

I know.

Don't know it. Live it.

Moravia's novel attempts to set the record straight so that Homer's name should appear above Freud's on the metaphorical marquee of history. Lang makes it as clear as the merging of sea and sky on Capri that Homer's world was real to Homer, and fights to preserve the spirit of The Odyssey *against the producer's vapid Freudianizing of Ulysses' reluctance to return*

      home.

On what grounds?

That Penelope never loved him anyway. And Lang wants to end on Odysseus' first sight of Ithaca.

2

Camille becomes contemptuous of her screenwriter husband
   instantaneously at Cinecittà.

(—Posters for *Hatari* on the crumbling walls.—)

But he deserves it for lamenting having married a "stupid 28 year old typist."

When Prokosch asks Camille to ride with him to his villa in his red Porsche
convertible, she   hesitates as if   waiting   for her husband   to say

"no, she'll ride with me," and when without hesitation despite her hint hint hint
he says "it's all right"   (*but how did he mean what he said?*)
she withdraws

all her love   Forever After   and substitutes for it contempt: distilled.

Like a potion you might carry in a vial.

A contagion of contempt.

Oh hell, her riding with the producer is just the last straw and fore-

shadows their doom.

How still their bodies are in the aftermath of their tawdry indelible death on the highway.

The bodies slumped pathetically, like a human version of roadkill. You don't see the crash; you hear it; at an eerie distance.

The second half was shot in Capri. Sea and sky were one. Jeweled turquoise.

But it was shot on the tawny sun-baked roof of the villa once owned by the fascist novelist Curzio Malaparte where he did his calisthenics every morning. And on the shaded paths through the woods.

Lovely rambles. Lost worlds. The sea pristine in spite of everything.

If the Fascists and Nazis were nothing if not physically fit, have you con-sidered that there might be something to consider about the American obsession with exercise.

Not in that way.

Although if Palance had a tantrum in the screening room . . . (Pause.) Is it apocryphal or true that Godard kept the camera running as the actor hurled a film can across the room like a discus thrower, wreck-ing footage and provoking Lang to comment on his breakthrough of feeling for Greek culture?

What provoked it?

Let's just say that what the producer saw in the rushes was not how he imagined the script on the screen.

Where history is concerned Lang saw far beyond his time.
In Metropolis, Mabuse, M.

Hitler loved *Metropolis* so much, with its alluring robots.

But hated M *and* The Testament of Dr. Mabuse *because he saw the Nazi soul reflected as, control-crazy, murderous, and insane.*

But the Führer counted on his own mesmeric powers to get Lang back on track and had Goebbels invite him to run the Third Reich's burgeoning film industry.

Lang fled for Paris that night, leaving everything behind.

He saw the system underneath the symptoms.

He may have even had a hand

in what eventually happened.

He called it so . . .

He was right on the die.

The lure of an eroticism that is unreal.

Inhuman.

Mind-control. Dr. Mabuse's misuse of his mental powers in a bizarre transmogrification of Schopenhaurian will.

His silent films symphonic.

His sound films monotonic . . . ; cruel.

American. In Hollywood he was a hired gun.

He made some good films with the scripts he was assigned.

And some great ones, like You Only Live Once *and, of course,* The Big Heat.

It is possible that Glenn Ford's super-normal policeman
who goes on a righteous rampage

after his wife is blown up by a car bomb
meant for him, is driven by Lang's rage

at Germany for everything and Hollywood
for taking away his freedom.

But he still languished less than Brecht in Los Angeles.

And they did get the chance to collaborate
on, of all things, a Western   [*Rancho Notorious*]
with a theme Lang chiefly loved: revenge.

3

B.B. (Bardot, not Brecht)
        confesses her fear of being
            bored in Capri.

I can imagine Brecht having the same fear of being bored in Venice.

B.B. *bored* in Venice?
He might not have bowed down before
Titian's "Annunciation" or genuflected
before every crucifix, but bored?

With intrigue behind every gargoyle?
He might have lost himself before a canvas,
seized on the tense silence
between the naked woman seated in coiling, mean-

looking weeds, nursing her child in the vulnerable open,
her gaze there to answer the gaze of the future;
and the well-turned-out soldier,
protector, potential assailant, voyeur,

appointed to stand across the creek—
both sides of the cleft root like two
question marks questioning each other—
his stare eternally unreturned.

He would have seen
fields in turmoil, distressed shepherds,
a rickety bridge the Romans would have X'd,
a lute when landscape required a flute.

And the lightning—shaped
like the wake of a mogul's speedboat—
signified a danger
not in nature but in history:

Venice under siege.
The end of pastoral.

♣

He would have given Casanova's memoirs
a political twist or plugged into the Romantics
who sought refuge and beauty and desired
change, getting past

pretty boy Shelley in the portraits,
to the Shelley who had fiber and fire;
the Shelley who could not rest when faced
with so much injustice, penned

"The Revolt of Islam" and that prose
fragment

The Assassins.

❧

Brecht could have done something in the vein of his *Coriolanus,*
only better

Revolt

with Leslie Howard as Shelley

unless his RAF plane had already been blasted out of the sky.

How do you know that B.B. wasn't nauseated by the thought of the author of the "Sensitive Plant?"

Because when he was living in exile in Los Angeles, he thought a lot about Hell and gathered that his "*brother* Shelley," in "Peter Bell," found it was a city much like London which inspired Brecht to base a poem on Shelley's, making his Hell the city of the fallen angels where the flowers grew as big as trees and needed constant and expensive watering.

You do remember the oddest . . .

I know.

Modest too.

Fatalistic really. And lucky, because my alumni card doesn't allow me to check books out and I can't stand

don't say it—"the delirious dust of stacks."

There were trees in the Baths of Caracalla when Severn portrayed Shelley writing *Prometheus Unbound.* Shelley found a stump on which to put his foot, and he found a footbridge over water.

Over where water once was, before Rome became a ruin.

Severn couldn't resist touching up his subjects; imbuing the dusk
with a light that never was: an impalpable purple.

But it could be Severn's idealization
that kept up the quality of care he offered,
martyr-like, to Keats, nursing him across turbulent seas

in the terminal stages of his terminal illness;
that gave him the spiritual strength
to endure the moment when Keats gasped

"Severn—I—lift me up—I am dying."

And as for sheer guts, Severn could have contracted tuberculosis from Keats just as Keats contracted it while nursing his brother Tom to his fevered end.

"AN EMBARRASSING DIGRESSION"

Forgive me but the mention of Leslie Howard makes me miss my father terribly.

You mentioned him.

Not I.

(Pause.)

It has to do with . . . another side . . . of my father . . . a sensitive and insightful and too little used part of his . . . too often brutal . . . nature. Leslie Howard's name had come up, who knows why, maybe apropos my seeing *Gone With the Wind* for the first time in Paris and being underwhelmed with both it and him.

Who?

Howard. I didn't see the point of Howard. Oh Ashley, Ashley . . . Howard was like a vapor, neither manly, forceful, or particularly handsome . . . when my father said—and I'm sure he was sober at the time—in a quiet and level voice, an intimate tone he only too rarely had access to, that *you'd have to look pretty far and wide to find another actor with Howard's particular appeal, that he was sensitive without being effeminate,* and I have to say that made me revise my opinion on the spot and instantly see *Leslie* Howard as being endowed with this particularly wonderful trait, a trait which I valued enough to feel embarrassed at not having recognized it myself for what it was, I mean . . . , why would I see Montgomery Clift's portrayal of Matthew Garth in *Red River* as the high point in movie acting and be numb dumb deaf and blind to the virtues of Howard, and Howard's Ashley, and now his last name is coming to me, Wilkes. Ashley Wilkes.

But there was another problem which my father couldn't have foreseen: that I didn't like most of the films Howard was in, like *Of Human Bondage,* trudge and groan, and

I can't believe it!

yes, even *Petrified Forest* and *Brief Encounter.* I didn't like them and don't plan to revise my opinion. The very knowledge that *Brief Encounter* is going to be shown once again on Public Television depresses me.

I'd rather see that one hour film that De Sica shot at the train station in Rome.

Hardly satisfying.

But raw. Raw.

Clift's wired jaw? Satchel full of painkillers?

Get off it.

But you might be persuaded to revise your estimation of Howard in Brief Encounter *if you're willing to take a reminder that it wasn't he but Trevor Howard who acted in that movie which you'll never like.*

Now that you mention it. Strange, until this instant my memory . . .

Your mother said it just the other day: **you always get everything wrong**. *You mention your cousins the Wolfs, claiming never to have set eyes on them in your life . . .*

only that I don't remember having met them

and then you misspell their name.

"OK Mom" I said, genuinely flummoxed, "how do you spell it."

"With two f's."

Can you believe it? Two fucking f's.

I can. Reality is inexhaustibly layered and the truth inexhaustibly difficult to attain.

Nothing is sadder to me than an insoluble situation like the one in *Brief Encounter.*

What's insoluble? They could have thrown away their previous lives and gone off into the sunset together, they could have chosen to change their lives and taken the responsibility that goes with it, especially when you have children, if either of the characters, (because frankly I don't remember either), had children.

Yeah.

Don't let it get you down.

Let's get back to the subject. I begin to find your Mr. Lang a bit . . . too much of a pundit. . . .

All that crap about man being
alone before
god, ship-
wrecked until god's
absence comes
to his
aid.

Thanks for averting "rescue."

But he doesn't stop there. Palance's Prokosch, a demented smirk on his face, asks his lackeys, his instantly replaceable screenwriter and director, to stop talking because he wants to share his vision: "I love gods." (Long pause.) "I know . . . just how they feel." But "Fritz" doesn't wait for the comical vacuity of this utterance to sink in; he puts in his two cents of vintage wisdom as if his producer cared.

"Don't forget, the gods have not/created men; men/have created gods."

He may quote from Holderlin but he sounds like Horace.

Cautionary words drive me up the wall.

Which makes me wonder . . . what would a . . . Horace . . . sound like if he were alive . . . in an age like ours? Would he run around giving good advice, like his later incarnation, Horatio, to those dudes on the parapets who are clueless enough to ask, vis-à-vis the ghost of Hamlet's father on that cliff that beetles over that base into the sea, "shall I strike at it with my partisan"? Or those bodiless creations ecstasy is very cunning in?

Have you forgotten again that error and misprision are our allies?

Speak then, I charge you.

I'll give it a go.

AGAINST ODDS AGAINST

There's nothing you can do, After Life,
to stanch the passage of time, or the wrack
it leaves behind, a wound for which all
    tourniquets are useless.

Everyone is forced to navigate
the river of the dead alone. It's futile
to excise a good twelve-hundred pound
    prize steer in offering

(from the herd rented at $10 a head even when they just
grazed while Hawks was dying for Rain Valley
to stop living up to its name so he could get *Red
River* shot before the cast mutinied)

to Pluto—who in this inferno restrains
tri-sexual Geryon on a leash of tricyclics . . . ,
or an empire builder like Tom Dunson,
    Matthew Garth's foster father.

There is no getting the better of a beast
who when you yell "go fuck yourself"
just asks for its hands to be unclasped;
    and never a way to escape

the brackish waters of backed-up Cocytos,
the infamous Danae and the all-too-famous
Sisyphus: thanks to one concise, timely essay
    by twenty-nine year old

Albert Camus. Maybe pushing a boulder
uphill forever isn't quite as onerous when the wind
is your father? There are more things on earth
    than making the best of the worst.

Wage war on war? Why not?
So long as everything comes to nothing.
And the wave-roar grows hoarse
        from breaking the news

to the deluded multitudes who go on
"wishing and hoping and hoping
and dreaming . . ." for Miracle
        Incorporated to rid

the sirocco of the germs it strews
cruelly, indifferently, on everyone
open to the wind, from tower-hidden kings
        to ragged beggars.

All that you have loved best will fall away.
The land you worked. The house you built.
The wife you loved. (The immense tenderness
        that grew between you.)

Alone, the invidious cypress will cast shadows
on your harvest's golden glow; then in no time at all
it will be time to set the field on fire:
        so the grain can die.

Why are time's prisoners in their meager
tenure on earth so often inured to the giant
strides that occurred in the quality of life
        while they lived.

Take heart that someone like yourself only—
(dare I say it?)—more . . . evolved . . . will depart the site
where your physical body decomposes
        underneath the humped

mound, determined to alter future legislation
as regards cremation. He knows what wines
are ready to be opened and where they are within
        the labyrinthine

cellar and, jangling the keys, descends.
Rest content. You were an experiment.
To what end "man is only beginning"
       to glean a direction.

                                        (*after Horace, Odes, Book II, 14*)

THE "REAL" REVOLT

> "16 aug 38, appalling to read poems by shelley (not to
> speak of ancient egyptian peasant songs from 3000 years
> ago) in which he laments oppression and exploitation. is
> this how they will read us, still oppressed and exploited,
> and will they say: was it already as bad as that?"
>
> BERTOLT BRECHT, *Journals 1934–1955*

After an afternoon of walking through ruins and trying to imagine
the wholeness before it was lost, we thread our way unknowingly
through the narrow and tortuous Via di Lorensi and find ourselves on
the Piazza Navona at nightfall. *Ragazzi* kick a soccer ball between the
Fontana del Moro and the Fontana dei Fiumi as if it were still the sta-
dium and racecourse Domitian had built something less than a hun-
dred years after Jesus is said to have died. An athlete himself, my own
kid complains about his feet and laments that he can't play soccer
with the other kids. Strange how context alters energy flow. Or is it
desire? There appears no way home across the Tiber to Trastevere and
the steep uphill steps other than to walk.

The piazza is so deserted I find it hard to believe that days before, on
the feast of the Epiphany, which Vico might have rejoiced in, it was
chockfull, thronged: carousels and painted balloons, silver balloons
with faces outlined in white, like the ghosts of all the political rallies
that have taken place there.

Disoriented, travel-weary, my eyes burn now as halogen lamps flare
and a camera crew appears, wanting to catch the light while it is still
in the act of vanishing, crepuscular. An aquiline actor, dressed in early
nineteenth century garb, waistcoat, ruffled shirtfront, the whole-bit,
mutters beside the fountain, and he is then interrupted by someone
who could be his hologram or double but in modern dress. I ask a
member of the crew as he opens up a fresh pack of *Lucky Strikes* what
the film is about and he answers in American-English that "It's a film
about Brecht writing a play about Shelley." "Can we watch?" "As long
as you don't cross over the chalk." Fatigue from wandering brings on

disconnected forms of wondering. The play may be the thing but I'm trying to remember the last time I saw a pack of *Lucky*'s in the U.S.A.

Shelley:

Who remembers the Roman wilderness
before Romulus forged refuges, transformed
crags into caves, fashioned dwellings
or ventured like Aeneas into the Lupercal cave?
Did the sublimely insightful German, in Los
Angeles, know that my "Peter Bell"
was a parody of another "Peter Bell," penned
by one W.W., whose hard-earned renown
for the great works written in his youth,
such as the 1805 version of *The Beginning*
worked inadvertently to eclipse
the generation after (the public being
somewhat limited as to what it can take in;
digest). It was enough for my generation
to carve a niche in the wake of Shakespeare,
Spenser, and Milton, but to contend
with a living monument's monumental
accomplishment, his alter-ego's
rapturous propaganda, "explaining
metaphysics to the nation"
while never failing to extol—
to his own disadvantage in the end!—
the pioneer's pioneering virtues—
was a bit much. . . . Are Byron, poor
John Keats and I mere standard bearers
for their "romantic movement" instead of
revolutionaries?

(Pauses.)

Originals!

(Pauses.)

I fear I have not expressed myself clearly.

It's that . . . that deadly duo takes up so much of
the available oxygen . . . , and I would
lay down my life for Lord
Byron, fiend, friend, incomparable gin
drinker, swimmer, and man of principles . . .

(With both hands he brushes back the forelock falling over his eyes.)

It's time to set the record straight,
to spring me from the preciosity trap,
to detach the words I took pains to compose
from the romantic images of me physically.

[Aside.] Besides, whatever the screenwriters who imagine they are
putting these very words into my mouth at this moment imagine,
David Herbert Lawrence was right to nail me for hailing that skylark
as a bird that never existed. And it's true that my images weren't
always precise. You'll remember that somewhat epicene Italophile
American novelist James, yes Henry James, said that Nathaniel
Hawthorne's flaws were the result of his isolation from the company
of other writers. Then think of a young exiled Englishman, on the
run with his wife and children, writing in every imaginable circum-
stance except "at a desk," in carriages, small boats, ruins like the
lovely, leafy baths of Caracalla which helped me to imagine myself
several millennia back in time in order to compose *Prometheus
Unbound.*

And yes yes YES even in my time we thought about genre and form
qua form. Shakespeare and Jonson wrote plays. Spenser and Milton
wrote epics, so that left a lot that was still undone in terms of lyrics
and odes and plays not meant to be performed.

Then there is the further question which it doesn't take a detective to
anticipate: if I really was committed to social change on a large scale
why was I so foolhardy? Why for example, after the squall during a
sailing expedition with Byron, that strong, skillful, and indefatigable
swimmer, the rudder broke and waves threatened to capsize the boat,
why, after this near death, which I faced incidentally with more
humiliation than fear, did I not

simply learn how to swim?

(Shelley now addresses the wild-haired man of about his age, thirty, dressed in a black leather jacket and blue jeans, who has assumed a stance beside him. And finished his sentence for him.)

Or build a boat with a keel deep enough to withstand riotous squalls . . . ?

Remember, I asked you.

And as far as Frankenstein's points of resemblance to myself . . .

♣

I begin to indulge in a somewhat absurd reverie in which the film-makers argue over how to portray Shelley, like Fritz Lang (as director), Jack Palance (as producer), and Michel Piccoli (as screenwriter) do with regard to their adaptation of *The Odyssey* in *Contempt.*

"I like the way Shelley sometimes utters a phrase with a German accent, but this is far too static. Why not show Shelley, during his tenure in Venice, playing pool with Byron à la 'Julian and Maddalo,' even have an overvoice reading some passages of the poem, or riding along the Lido . . ."

"I don't like that 'tenure.'"

"Sojourn then."

"Let's take advantage of the fact that Shelley and Byron were obsessed with being by, near, or preferably—weather being the least of their concerns—on the water."

"Ok, and let's use color for the urban scenes and black and white for the seaside at Le Spezia."

"I won't say no, but why?"

"To leech out that damn romantic image that perpetuates the perpetual misunderstandings about our subject who had to have been tough, strong-willed, and disciplined to accomplish what he did in so short a time. Also, B.B. would have approved."

"I won't say no. But a leeched out sepia might be even better for the hazy olive-grays of the Tuscan hills and seaside scenes in Le Spezia than straight black-and-white."

"Yeah. Considering he composed with his notebook on his knee— hillsides and boats were his desk—and we already decided that Severn's prettified image of him in the Baths of Caracalla was not only misconceived but ultimately revolting. Sure, little Johnny Keats could compose an entire ode in an hour on Dilke's porch while nightingales were trilling, but it can get messy in the open air, far from anything either you or I would designate as shelter. No offense to Severn the man. I still break down when I think of how he cared for Keats."

"He might have been no more than 5'2, but being fearless, burly but not stout, he could have kicked your butt. He would have flown at your throat for that remark."

(Scene: the real *Revolt* in progress on the real Piazza Navona)

Shelley:

We boarded the packet boat from Dover to Calais in heavy weather.

You daring denizens of cocktail-shaker whirring blender Hovercrafts and ferries are clueless as to what dangers any travel threatened to procure.

(The man of the present interrupts.)

I suppose you're coming to the part about you, Mary, and Claire as a threesome. Did the two women . . . you know? And where were the sleeping children, and what if one woke crying? Did you have conjugal relations with Mary and find Claire at the door, wondering if she could join

you, and touch Mary with her tongue while she was in a relaxed state
and let her gently return the favors, so that you groaned from her precise
somnambulistic groping, woman to woman. You both reviled voyeurism
and believed love was to be shared. You would enter Claire from one end
and Mary from the other. Her fingers and yours would meet and Claire
would raise her right leg and when you came, always too soon, Mary
would continue, probing, spreading, licking . . . and groaning, oh, oh, as
if with relief, like someone sighing finally after an arduous . . .

(Shelley looks at him as if appalled by the invasiveness of his question,
clutches his side—his famous "Mephitic pain" returning—and strug-
gles to continue. The director yells cut and suddenly the group is in a
huddle, including several other actors, at least two of whom are
women, in early nineteenth century dress. The director calls "roll
'em." Shelley now moves his hand along the fountain's rim as he
speaks and lights flood the rockwork and grottoes.)

While we three, Mary, Claire, and I leaned on the deck rail
(and Claire was not impervious to the mountainous
waves), a soldier's wife, hysterical,
recited the Lord's Prayer and threw up
at the same time.

Forgetfulness is the bane of history.
What history? Where? I know: body-counts.
But what does knowing how many people
were lost on a given day have to do with history?

Shakespeare portrays Achilles as a heel.
(Albeit in a play I find it hard to believe he wrote.)

A non-sequitur? What else is history?
History. History invents itself as it goes along.
But whatever was may exist in some hard eternal form.
Still intact. A kernel of its former self.

How each generation construes . . . consecutive thought
wearies poor creatures given to taking
rhythmic dictation from the wind—
but take the professional historians who argue

there never was a holocaust.

Outrageous? But if others have supported their premises
while numbered survivors are still alive to testify
otherwise, what happens when no one from that era
with stamped wrists remains?

Impossible?

I would have thought so. Yesterday.

Do you think you can accurately reimagine
what antiquity was really like by hiring NASA
planes to fly over and take photographs
that can reach ten meters below the soil?

Do you think I expect an answer?

But none of us are loveable eccentrics.

We're drawn to mimicry.

(Clears his throat.)

To set the record straight
I cadged my German accent from Coleridge,
who, though not bad at imitating others himself,
not to say copying, ruined
his mind there. And only ceased from posing
unanswerable questions when walking
fens no one had traversed before without
any fear of getting lost in the real,
jotting down—phrases—broken by—dashes—
where the poems it is assumed
he never wrote lay buried in a log
he never thought to quarry for its gems. . . .

And now I am stricken with a sad thought,
despite my enmity toward S.T.C
& Co., that if his most significant

male mother, I mean other, had been someone
more like Pound   than   that   ...   cold Cumberland,
who preferred landscapes and animals to people,
he might have undergone a second birth.

But to think that William the Sublime
would take an active interest in his friend's real work
is as fantastical as the poem he unconscionably excised
from the *Lyrical Ballads*, "Christabel"—
delivering a psychic knockout punch
to his despondent partner,
whose desire for his hero's approval
had no bound.
William was a man who could cast his nets
effortlessly backward and bring the dead
years and events back to life more vividly
than life allows.
Samuel was a man who agonized over the instant
he was in and sometimes—hit upon solutions.
Being disabled in the lime-tree bower
appealed to him (—don't ask me why
I'm one for vast expanses myself)—
unless physical limits enabled him to focus,
do one thing at a time and abandon
manic projects.
It's as if Wordsworth sensed that this
innovative poem, "founded on a new
principle," to count in each line
"the accents, not the syllables,"
springing rhythm free from rigid numbers,
could throw too much attention
on his blocked, burdened
beyond measure, forever
beleagured and uncertain
collaborator.

(Pause. Stares into space.)

Or maybe the two men were one
and their symbiosis is beyond
analysis.

                          ♣

To run his hand along the fountain's rim he'd have to be seated. It makes more sense for Shelley first to be seen standing before the Fontana del Moro, deep in meditation beside the statue of "The Moor," which can then lead him to say more about Shakespeare.

"Maybe he should look up at the statue, even if he is more of a marine divinity than an homage to Othello, with a wicked leer, point to the Ethiopian and say something like 'you know I hate the Moor.'"

Shelley:

I wonder if they're right, the distracted
multitudes who claim the bard had never
been to Venice. It's difficult to catch
the ambiance: think of my lines evoking
this hazy, harsh, sweet atmosphere,
without the author having spent time in
Tuscany or on the Palatine
much less in a labyrinth like Venice. . . .
I'm not in Venice now, am I Gian Lorenzo?
You're my witness if I have one. Or none.
If I address you by your first name, know
that I admire your way with marble
even if the line itself is a little
too . . . too . . . do I have to say it?—
sham-ful for my tastes.

And then immediately switch roles and speak as the moor. Something like

Shelley:

Ah, sweet to have been a man of action,
a soldier, who could define his life

30

in terms of what he had done and then win
the woman's love, like Othello's escape
from the imminent deadly breach. . . . Simple
enough, unless some betrayer turns his mind
irrevocably around and around.

I realized that the whole scene would be better accomplished with
montage, a rapid series of shots lasting no more than two seconds
each: first an aerial view of the piazza as a whole; then a flashback, giv-
ing a stereoscopic image of history, jousts, races, nobles watching
from their carriages; then a reverse angle shot, from the bottom of the
Fountain of the Rivers to the Egyptian-style Roman obelisk on top of
the fountain against a bottomless sky . . . ; then to an empty square at
nightfall with a few pigeons on and around the fountains; then
another flashback to a Christmas feast with the camera closing in on
the miniature Christmas cribs; then to a mock naval battle going on
in the days when they used to flood this piazza made for metamor-
phosis; to a contemporary feast of the Epiphany ending on a close-up
of the "silver balloons with faces outlined in white," which I so
recently witnessed, like the ghost of political rallies past.

And after we cut from him addressing the statue of the moor I'd have
him standing in the Fountain of the Rivers, his hand cupped to his
ear.

Shelley:

You'd have me get my feet wet at nightfall
would you Gian Lorenzo? Fine. But it is
all right with you and your ghost if I walk
through the grotto where all four rivers meet?
Maybe you should put that lion on a leash
when I pass from the Ganges to the Danube.

There are limits to what the dead can do.

"Many harsh words have been written about Shelley."

"Like that crack of Lawrence's vis-à-vis the bodiless idealism of 'bird that never wert.'"

"'Peter Bell the Third' must have hit Brecht like a bombshell."

"Jean Seberg would have made a fine Mary Shelley."

"I like that 'would have.' Can we stick to real possibilities?"

"Los Angeles was good enough for Thomas Mann but not Brecht . . ."

"Mann lived in Venice. Venice is way beautiful. Gulls wheel over the piers."

"Figures. That closet-queen banker with his cartload of metaphysics knew how to transform exile into domicile."

"It was like he had a license to hide."

"Why don't we let the camera zoom in on that lion's head."

"Better he should be riding the horse and after the entire scene has run its course of course cut to him riding on the Lido with Byron."

"But these are compatible ideas. We can do the marble lion's head and then the flesh and fur horse. (Pause.) But why have Shelley in nineteenth century dress when in a church no more than a good" (stands up and pretends to be swinging a golf club) "four iron away" (finishes swing and pretends to be watching shot on the follow through), "from Bernini's fountain, San Luigi dei Francese, there's a triptych by Caravaggio of St Matthew which is set in the Rome of 1600 or thereabouts."

"Not more art!"

"Hear me out; he's a forerunner of 3-D. Without Caravaggio, no *Murder in the Wax Museum.*"

(The writers and crew, within hearing range, half-giddy from sleep deprivation, boredom and overstimulation, burst into spontaneous laughter.)

"Do they hand out the glasses or do you have to bring your own?"

"Look, we've all reached our limit, but no one asked you to accept this . . . line of work. And if you accepted the oblique allusion to Matthew Garth why cancel out another representation that will free us up, I promise you, in the long run. So listen: there's Matt seated among the taxmen with Jesus at the far end sayin' (I'm sure some of you know the story far better than I) 'come on, it's time to meet your destiny' before your eye follows the story left to right to the other two canvases with their angels and killers. And everyone's dressed in the Elizabethan ruff of 1600 A.D., not the usual approximations of what these people wore in the year . . . zero."

"What are you driving at?"

"That it works and I see no reason why for the purposes of this film that Shelley, our Shelley, shouldn't be dressed like his doppelganger or those other aging ageless raggedish student-types hangin' out in the square while we . . . film around them."

"Why can't we do both? Otherwise how separate Shelley from his double?"

"Because that interrogator isn't really his double: he's just relatively the same age and build."

My *ragazzo* now groans with fatigue. And this sound, far more intense than his complaining, rouses me to lead us through the zigzag into a perilous traffic jam via Via della Cuccagna, distracting ragazzo from distraction, (transcending all physical exhaustion), like belts and wallets, and grab the first Roman taxi I have taken except to and from the airport or train station. Inside, I continue my reverie about the filmic possibilities of *Revolt*.

(Scene: The camera follows Shelley through the streets until he reaches the Campo dei Fiori and Giordano Bruno's statue. As Shelley approaches the statue in silence the camera backs away until he disappears into the crowd. Cut to long shot from an aerial height of the adjacent Campo and Piazza. Cut to a long take of an ordinary morning on the Campo when it becomes an immensely colorful marketplace. Camera should focus on the vivid fruits and vegetables, as if to affirm something human that persists in spite of all the questions and complications that the film introduces.)

Immense relief when my backpack hits the floor of our apartment. As I hit the sofa an image balloons of Brecht in exile thinking about his "brother" Shelley. I open the five-colored Clairefontaine notebook Karen sent me from New York when I was in Vermont, and come across this quotation from B.B's *Journals* "20 mar 47, finish THE ANACHRONISTIC PROCESSION, a kind of paraphrase of shelley's *the masque of anarchy*." The *ragazzo* assumes a position beside me on the long white sofa and while, from the Gianicolo's heights we watch fog cover the domes and terra cotta roofs, he covers a page in his new spiral notebook, ("*Carta riciclata ecologica*,") beginning with the sentence: "That bridge over the Tiber we crossed today was built on the first day of the world."

BRECHT LOOKS AT XERISCAPING
WITH A THOUGHT ABOUT SHELLEY

The houses of these happy souls
Are empty even though they "live" in them.
No one ever said the houses in Hell

Are ugly; but, the masked faces
Who dwell therein are as fearful
Of destitution as the poor.

Rain isn't good enough for the gardens
Of privilege. If flowers
Are to grow as big as

Trees they require "solutions"
That cost more to mix and import than I can
Think about without—exploding.

A man's a man. And money's money.
So why be driven into a toil just because
It costs more to water one lawn in Hell

Than entire towns along the The Black Forest
Where I wandered in my mother's womb;
Where I learned, despite the primeval chill

That will be in my bones until I meet my end—
To somehow survive anywhere,
Even exiled in Hell.

I'd like to bulldoze an actor's xeriscaped backyard.
I'd like to knock the bloody sod down
For mocking the folk wisdom that "a man's home

Is his castle" by erecting his own real imitation
Castle, moat and all,
And wreck it with a wrecking ball.

But I can't: not when, driving in my own
Comfortable car, I hadn't yet recovered
From the shock of having denied

A bedraggled tramp's polite—
(Now I'll never break free of Fritz
Lang's determinist tyranny and collaborate

With Preston Sturges if the "bum" was
Joel McCrea researching his role
In *Sullivan's Travels!*)—

Request for a ride on a rainy road at nightfall,
By snapping: "we're not in
The service business." Everyone's

Complicit. Even if I was possessed
By one of my own caricatures of greed,
I'm not about now to pass

Judgment on Gide for contemplating his plane
Tree's admirable qualities
In the occupied zone

During these darkening times,
While I luxuriate in his wartime journals
In far-off, "sunny, Californ-i-a-yay."

THE ASSASSINS

Now you must be proud of yourself that your meditation on assassins on behalf of your friend's obsession with hit men

and the prose fragment of Shelley's I hadn't known existed that takes
   its cue from the *hassasin*, the Islamic sect for whom getting stoned
   on hash(ish)—
the root of assassin—
was inseparable from their desire and license to kill

has culminated in a death that strikes only too close to home.

The desert.

I can't seem to stop replaying a song
Emmy Lou Harris talk-chant-sings her way through,
"Jerusalem Tomorrow," as if she
had to call on all of her resources;
not the entire piece so much as the
marvelous dark light she throws on the line

"Well I'm in this desert town and it's hot as hell."

I'm not saying I was the Israeli Prime Minister's fan—I'm not saying I'm not. But the relentless bombings that continue in the wake of his death sicken sleep.

Heaven—is distressed. The counsels of the gods
are sequestered in severe consultation.
I was on the brink of pride yesterday when I listened in
on your long distance powwow with that young man
whose first name is a letter,
like Mr. Bond's co-secret-service-workers, "M." and "Q.,"
(some friends you have!), and heard you connect
those merciless mercenaries, "hit men"—

*a far too dignified term for that **scum**—*

first with that secret order of Moslems
for whom killing was the highest act and
the killer accorded a status more
fitting for saints and maryrs . . .

—and how could someone I consider my own son
be so far off the mark?—"the roots of"
ha ha, "existential thinking," I mean come on

how can you compare

the killers of Montherlant and Gide and Malraux

let's not forget Camus and Melville

Melville?

Jean-Pierre, *Le Samurai,* the director whom Jean
Seberg interviews in the airport in *Breathless*
and asks him how many women
a man can love and he can't stop counting.

Ok, but why Camus . . . ?

Mersault on the beach. The dizzying light and heat.
His eyes sting from the downpour of his own salty sweat.
And in the rain of fire after the sky cracks open he
squeezes the trigger; no, it gives way, almost as a reflex,
as if guns could speak and this one said
"shooting is my métier, I willed his finger to move,"
but it was a man who then fired off four
extra shots, which seemed to sink,
like something out of special effects,
into the Arab's flesh without a trace.
He hadn't moved a muscle; he could have been
a candidate for morgue duty already;
and who could have seen so far ahead as to guess
that each successive shot was a knock
on the door of his death sentence.

Oh hell, all these motiveless murders come out of the French taking Ivan Karamazov's "everything is permitted" a little too literally, like that passage in Gide's Lafcadio's Adventures.

No no no. Gide never had an original idea. Lafcadio is Kirilov's shadow.

Kirilov?

The character in *The Possessed* whose suicide is the first real gratuitous act.

But if he envisions suicide as the only way in which he can become God, it isn't entirely motiveless.

Maybe not. There are many routes around this question.

("L'acte gratuit")

There is the one moment whose purity brings on
a kind of ecstasy, when Lafcadio, for no reason at all—

except to destroy the gulf between the imagination and the deed—
corridor curtains drawn, train rumbling over a bridge,

pushes that dimwit seated next to him on the train, off
the train, when to break his fall the victim-to-be

grips the back of the anti-hero's head like a claw
and leaves him holding his cuff.

*Ah, maybe destiny has a role in the way
perfection eludes the criminal.*

Yeah, in *The Getaway*, the insouciant Doc McCoy
was sure he'd put a bullet through his cretinous partner's heart
and watched him die his well-deserved death in a creekbed,
which proves that even those who are best known for never
making mistakes, make mistakes.

And error is not the aid to the man of action that it is to the artist and the thinker. And these men often feel that they deserve to die for their mistakes, as if imperfection made them unworthy to live.

The fact that your Mr. Bond—and I don't give your blood father high marks for taking you to Dr. No the day it opened—has a license to kill and uses it to get to evil Mabusian characters doesn't make him any less of a killer in god's eyes.

What would there be to kill in the world if not murder itself.

Let's move to higher ground. Pretend that Shelley's formidable future in-laws, William Godwin and Mary Wollstonecraft, had questioned your interest in assassins. You be Shelley and I'll be Mary's parents.

Shelley:

"My assassins derive from a small
community of speculators who flourished

away from society's conventions
after they survived the sack of Rome

harming no one until roused to kill
avenging Crusaders and who, once compelled

to reinvent society from scratch
without concession to what the known world

called "society," lived together in
near miraculous harmony . . ."

Godwin:

"So they weren't sheerly vicious killers."

Shelley:

"No, but when crossed, as is true of many
pure and noble natures who incline,

like Luther himself, toward all or nothing they became
ferocious and cut the throats of

any enemy without remorse or guilt.
They never hesitated."

"You make them sound like professionals. Like hit men."
"Whom they do amazingly resemble.

They didn't think of life and death as having value
apart from the specific qualities that made life life."

Godwin:

"This is worthwhile Percy, try and finish this one."
"These *hashishin* were hardly flower-children."

Oh my god.

What?

*Godwin's response reminded me that his daughter was responsible for
Doctor Frankenstein, and since there's probably some connection between
that monster and Doctor Mabuse, I may have been too harsh in the way I
spoke to you about your, your . . .*

Now you've been seized too.

I'll recover.

No one recovers, they just stop feeling the sensation or pain, or they
forget.

Maybe I should look back, maybe I've missed . . .

There'll be time for that. In the meantime, rest.

*I think I will. My stamina isn't . . . , and god knows heaven isn't rife with
stimulants.*

And you always were the world's lightest sleeper.

Always, always.

You sound sad. And this mild attack of contrition is so unlike you.

I've nothing to say. Are you familiar with the word "change"?

———

Here the word is never used, even over cribbage.
Here everything is repetition.
The dead depend on the living more than they want.

A WINTER NIGHT IN THE
CITY OF GOD

"Rome, a dark jungle, a good place to hide."
MARCELLO in *La Dolce Vita*

But as so often happens when you find yourself going down the wrong
   path
following ludicrous, ridiculous, even illicit leads

something almost always seems to intervene,
like a kind of internal Lone Ranger,
to break up, bash to pieces your reverie
which could be closer to that of the hassissin—

than even you would wish.

It's true, but it happens so strangely.

How strangely?

There I am wandering around Rome.

You mean roaming The Eternal City.

You make me sound like a cat.

Strange that you should introduce that phrase at this moment?

(Pause.)

Why strangely you say?

I was waiting for you to ask.

Life has no time to waste.

Then why should it waste so much of everything else?

Try The City of God *as a synonym.*

To you it is a city; to me, intoxicated by toxic gasoline fumes and cigarette smoke (until my lungs signal me to leave)—as well as a garden with palm fronds, umbrella pines, decapitated statues, soccer fields, waterfalls, a maze, a casino and views ranging from EUR to Vatican City—it is a savannah.

You're in the park once you pass under the ancient arch, but you must go down the long gravel path, past the staggered torsos, before you're really in the garden. My first time in I stayed until night and the rain began to fall simultaneously and I had crossed over some invisible boundary from where everything I had just seen had disappeared from view. I headed for the first exit. The first couple I encountered said it was at least eight miles to my point of origin if I continued on city streets. "But if it was only two miles to here . . . " The man made circuitous circles with his forefinger. "Thanks," I muttered, disheartened. "You're better off going back the way you came." "I see that." Wet, cold, lost and hungry, I wandered onto a grassy knoll, where I saw three young people, two men and a woman, moving in my direction with slow and easy strides. I waved. They waved back. They told me what markers to look for to retrace my steps and offered me a joint. I said I'd love to if I weren't lost, and was too proud to ask him to repeat the directions since I remembered only the most general ones—such as where I made the wrong turn that brought me to this place, and "once you can see the casino you are home free."

And when you were home free?

I stopped at the cafe nearest to my apartment and downed several espressos laced with grappa. The owner noticed how ragged I was and asked to hear what happened. A small crowd gathered while I told him the story. An American painter was at the bar, clearly amused by the interest and good will for which I was more grateful than I wanted to reveal. "They seem to like you here," she said, "and you'll never get lost in that park again." "You've lost me there." "The hypocanthus. It's evolutionary."

I continue to get lost daily, but without the nervousness. I make a point of getting into bed no later than 2 AM but rarely get to sleep

long before the sky, approaching dawn, is gray, and wake, to a vicious
inner alarm clock at 7:53, sniffing, roaming the apartment like a lair,
almost afraid to open the shutters to the unanswerable blast of light.

Leave it to you not to have venetian blinds.
And you never were an early riser.

It's not just the light, it's vapors and smells
that incite me to rise even though I'm desperate
for rest and hurry to the cafe to catch

Rome on the prowl with a restless
beautifully purposeless fervor,

destinies never in for questioning,

before the senses are numbed
by the imminent influx of habitués
arriving on growling motorcycles,

which make up in noise what they lack in horsepower,

converging on the cafe,
the near empty space suddenly flooded with cool
cats who light up their filterless Camels in unison
and blow smoke into each other's faces
with the intensity of a lifeguard
giving artificial respiration to a rescued child.

When you said "savannah" I thought you were leading up
to marshes, grassy planes, wild animals grazing . . .

It's more of a wager that whatever
draws me now also drew the Etruscans.
What permeates the air now is not far
from what the Etruscans experienced
upon waking. The differences are more
bound up with progress and appearances:
changes in apparel, the use of cars
instead of carriages. Because the same

spirits emanate. Which explains nothing
less than everything. Aqueducts took care
of a major worry and once beyond
survival abstract possibilities
asserted themselves and led to the rise
and fall of *The Glory and the Gory.*

But this isn't what drew the Etruscans.
They didn't calculate their migration
from the Po along the Appian Way
to the campagna; they were drawn
by the same insensible force.

Man is an animal.

Strange that you should have chosen that book. Because during the
dire summer I spent at your apartment in Colorado Springs, I read a
novel called *The Half Gods*, and called the author in Santa Fe. . . . A
few years later we connected in New York City during a lecture he'd
given on Blake.

Why not after? What did you do, interrupt?

It was a seminar. He asked for questions. And at dinner that night he
said the *City of God* was the most important book he'd ever read.

But that still doesn't contradict my assertion. By God I'd bet a bottle of
Jack Daniels *that you've never read that. And where did this "discussion"*
take place?

In our railroad flat on 89th St. between Lex and Third.

Now that's going back in time. You weren't there long enough for me to
set foot . . .

I don't know that you would have wanted to. Even before the fire. We
spent the year rent-free as caretakers for a 200 year old house in
Duchess County. Anyway, this man whose first name was the same as
that of my real father, and whose last name had a decisive ring to it,
thought it a major tragedy and symptom that everyone read chapters

x, q, and k (especially "k") of *The Confessions* while no one ever
cracked *The City of God* anymore . . .

I like that "cracked." Your blood father used to break the spine of every
new book you showed him. Proceed.

I will obey, were you ten times my father.

This very day, after the incident I haven't yet set down,
a friend loaned me a book I claimed I couldn't find
in Manhattan where he'd found it . . .

swear! If you loved your "little rabbi"
and more importantly your true spiritual father
then commit to the positions which you embrace
despite your dialectics.

It's 3 AM Italian time.
My resistance is breaking down.
along with my Duracell batteries.
I'd swear the book about the ragazzi is "OP"

You lost me there. Swear by my shofar.

Out of print in English, I'm sure it is, A *Violent Life* . . . ,

Swear?

I haven't checked Books in Print if that's what you . . .

Then why "swear," why not bet, or guess?

Your advice no sooner uttered than accepted.

Even conjecture.

Swear.

I have sworn't.

There's no question that after Chicago
my pulpits were in backwaters—I'll bet
I could count on the fingers of one hand
the people with whom I could discuss ideas.
But I did subscribe to Commentary
and Time, *and saw his* Gospel of St. Matthew
while you were an ungovernable teen,
who would never have gone to an art film
with a religious theme . . . and subtitles . . .

who knew nothing about nothing except

how to get away with murder.

Say'st thou so. Murder most foul!

The book's by one Pasolini, Pier Paolo.
The longest chapter is "Night in the City of God,"
while, as if to vindicate both perspectives,
the final chapter is called "The Eternal Hunger."

Go on, I like how he gets in both ideas without strain.

These *ragazzi di vita* hang in the same slums on the outskirts near
Ostia where Pier Paolo was born and died . . . ,
was, that is, murdered, run over

again again and again until his heart bore the mark
of tire treads, this a man who had the ingenuity and nerve
to make a road movie whose Italian title
forces the human vocal chords to mimic those of the birds
in the Franciscan sequence,

Uccellacci e Uccellini

(and whose name in our more guttural language,
Hawks and Sparrows, demands a clear throat to pronounce).

There's the loquacious raven,
the third who walked beside the once renowned—

48

now down and out
clown, Toto, and a then unknown
teenage actor, Ninetto.

The raven, (whose lines Pasolini recited),
spouted outdated Marxist maxims,
while his fellow travelers—cast as father and son—
were consumed with Saint Francis, sex and food:
in that disorder.

I regret that on our Sunday dash to Ostia Antica,
the site, (not weekend getaway "Ostia-by-the-Sea"),

with our American friend Miranda frenetic behind the wheel—
while her immobilized Italian husband,
whose heart is barely functioning at all,
jealous, desperate, hysterical,

rings her back the moment after
she hangs up the cell phone—I didn't dare

suggest a small detour to Idascalo
and the monument to Pier Paolo:

"maybe we could pass by
so I could offer a small prayer."

No, that wouldn't have stopped me:
it was Madelaine cramped in the back seat with the three boys
burning, dying to fling their overheated bodies
into the sea.

I couldn't imagine them being enticed by any offer
that meant another minute on the highway, such as:.
"a little further and we're in Etruria,
the boys can cool off in the swift running streams
and at nightfall witness the riders—
forty men and women on horseback
burst like thunder over the distant hill,

still wet and snorting after their dip
in the riverbed."

No matter. There are times when another hour
cooped up in a vehicle means
passing up the greatest site that ever breathed.
And that's all right.

Life before sites.

And the raven?

I hoped you wouldn't ask, for he ended
not where he eats, but where he was eaten

by the starving duo; his bones
scattered while the two

intrepid travelers reassumed their parabola
down the road of life. Emptiness, dust.

Requiring a clown? For relief from?

Ragazzi had become a beloved word which I used a lot
while my *ragazzo* was here, having turned in his baseball hat
for a Venetian beret with its charming question
where a logo would have been:

WHISKY
O
COCA?

*Son, I can tell that you miss your son, but give yourself another night
before you jump off a bridge.*

I'm not used to . . .

Can you get Jack Daniels *in the Gianicolo?*

Maybe, for like 45,000 . . . (lire).

Which is no more than your neo-epicurean buddies
will pay for an ephemeral bottle of Cognoscenti Dura
that's finished before the first course.

Your point?

Locate some Liquore Centerba Toro, *a greenish liquid made of a hun-*
dred herbs.

I had it once before, at around three
in the morning, after sampling a stream
of other exotic aperitifs and digestifs,
with a psychoanalyst who I first met
when I was fifteen and he had no room
for any new patients anyway and I wouldn't let
anyone tell me I didn't want to finish high school
in the Sonoran desert and not the smothering
green bower easterners mistook for the real.
Four years later I was just as stubborn.
But I had come east. And when I told him
what I wanted to do with my life and waited
for him to echo my father's predictions of doom

he addressed only how it might be done.

Older?

Four times my age when we met.
Twice my age now.

That's older than I ever got to be!
And you got on my case about the bourbon!
Never, never, would you consent
to a highball when I offered.

The alimentary in the Gianicolo had no *Jack*
in stock, and while the boss commanded
his minions to climb ladders

to case the high shelves he kept trying
to pawn off *Averno* as *Centerba*
through repetition of *herb.*
But I persisted.

Pour by your glass.

You don't have to push.

I was on the border of bliss
until, walking the Palatine
this warm day in mid-January,
the acacias had broken into blossom
and I was . . . disheartened . . . and alarmed
to discover that my vestigial asthma
had resurfaced with more force
than it has had since I was seven
and living in fear of suffocation in Chicago . . . ,

but there was a thermal inversion
in the eternal city and my breathlessness
was at least somewhat, thank god, normalissimo,
at least naturalissimo,
meaning: I wasn't ALONE in suffering.

(Pause.)

How that phrase of Pavese's haunts me tonight, "l'uomo solo."

Pour by my soul!

I have poured by your shofar.

Pour!

I have poured it. It's not the alcohol;
it's the calories: I need to lose half
the twenty pounds I've put on since you died.

At least my memory has outlived my life by more than half a year.

(Pause.)

Oh hell you were skin and bones. All angles.
You've got muscles. (Pause.) Besides, it may have been
the life-threatening brain-fever you contracted, later
in the summer of my death that made you want
to give the world and yourself the assurance
that you'll continue to take up
space
on the green
planet.

That's generous.

No, destiny. But the living are all
distracted from the whole by the part; and
from the eternal by the temporal.

From the *City of God* by wild lifestyles,
destitution, riches: an itch, an ache?

Don't think it escaped me—nothing
       does, that while you traversed
the Vatican with your oh so Christian
       wife, that you were drawn,
inexorably, to Raphael's portrayal of
       Genesis, early on;
I saw you return and return
       to the enigmatic version
of our flight from Egypt and
       the super-vivid foregrounded—
(in the right-hand corner)—
       Abraham and Isaac.
Don't be ashamed, son.
       You followed some
invisible intuition. I take
       no credit. You were drawn
to mystery; ambiguity.
       Questioning.

OK father. I think I understand
        what you're driving at.
I'm always surprised to be moved
        by Raphael,
but his Isaiah did it again.

What was the incident?

Back to that after this?

Ghosts don't become querulous until dawn.
And you've no reason
to back away now that your family
is thousands of miles away
and in another country.

Live by the day.

Did I hear you quote a Roman source?

I've no quarrel with Horace or any man who is
willing to change—as when that wolf
surprised him in the woods
and he didn't move to attack
and neither did the wolf.

And I know you know these sayings
were first set down in the Psalms, and the Song
of Songs, but not why you cite them elsewhere . . .

There isn't all that much to say.

My brains are addled.

How many Centerba's?

No more than three.

What proof?

I don't know.

You don't know. That's you. That's my ragazzo.

I didn't listen as the wine-sellers
chanted *forte, forte, forte,* I thought
forte si, forte big deal, I understand
forte, hard whiskey is forte, wine is not.
But now I see—though I can hardly stand—
that *forte* meant 70% alcohol, not 70 proof.

That's progress.

But crossing another campo around midnight in the best of moods,
I can't help but be sickened to see these words

**SIONISTI
ASSASSINI**

painted in white on the gray
wall, with the six-pointed Jewish star   below it
ruining   the joyful   night   and bringing back

the swastikas I noted here on the Gianicolo

and the faint   strains   of the anti-Semitic songs sung at Sunday's
    soccer game.

I hope you redeemed the night.

Another Rider

On a long unintentional digression I arrived, late,
on unfamiliar streets and my eventual loop toward the Gianicolo
left me with another trek around circular ruins.

Caving in from exhaustion, having not yet discerned
the shortcut up the steps through the dark copse,
I asked a young woman—passing on a Honda

at a temperate speed and dressed like a cat burglar
(but for her yellow helmet)—
for directions and, sighing, added "what about a lift?"

Her cycle was too small she said. By then I was half-on,
and she said "we can try," but when I reached
around her for the handlebars she said

"no, around my waist." I loved her matter of fact
manner and the way she gunned her cycle around the curves.
When I told her we had passed where I was staying

and she braked I asked if she wanted a drink.
"I would like to," she said, but that if she did she would
"fall down and never get home," having

worked all day and "just come from the gym."
Pavese came to my aid; when I muttered
"lavorare stanca," she answered, "si."

By the time I mentioned how well she spoke
English she had to yell "thanks!" as she vanished into the night's
black light.

II

THE DESERT OF EMPIRE

Withdrawn, always secretive, Venice was playing at hiding its true face once more, smiling impersonally at the hope that on a propitious day and hour it will show its real self to the good traveler as a recompense for his faithfulness.

JULIO CORTAZAR

PROVOKED IN VENICE

I

The 9:20 train from Arezzo to Venice via Florence.

Good-bye to Siena, and the glow of electric lights and fireflies in the night sky above the ancient parapets and the terra cotta condos and the black canopies of the umbrella pines.

The girl across from me on the train, her skirt riding higher with each stop. As noon approaches, she drowses over *Centi anni di solitudine* and lifts her pale face toward the sun; toward life.

How were Piero's frescoes?

Mostly destroyed, or worn away, and yet impeccably preserved in reproductions. . . . How?

Infra-red photography?

But how can that which has been effaced retain its color?

Do we live in a world in which the fake is an actual improvement over the real, like the Palenque at the Anthropology Museum in Mexico City, where you get the idea without the flies?

Maybe a child yelling out for a *Calypo* in a cafe at 9 in the morning is a welcome antidote to the somber, sober faces ordering coal-black espresso and staring into the doom-haunted pages of *Le Nazione*, or *The Guardian* . . .

Rome in grainy black and white; Siena in sepia; Venice in color.

But you haven't yet been here in winter, when the cold, hard winds come down from the mountains, and the water gets rough, and waves flood the piazzas.

The fog rolls in. You can't watch your back. You can't see the Lido,

San Erasmo, or the cypresses on the cemetery island of Francesco del Deserto. You're at the mercy of echoing footsteps, the creepy silence of the gondolas on the inner canals and, as a non-native Venetian crossing humpbacked bridges and moving through streets and alleys tense as corridors, you're praying that it's just someone

HARMLESS TO OTHERS
LIKE YOURSELF . . .

someone who . . . would be more prone to fall back or faint rather than approach and attack.

You wouldn't believe the sieges this city has withstood. You Americans are at a loss when devastation comes around, having no blood on the ground.

No points for the Civil War? When was the last time you spent an afternoon at Antietam and pondered the thousands who went to their graves in one day?

♣

What cannot be effaced, erased, or reproduced, is experience. Falling apart from fatigue a mere hundred yards shy of the hilltop fort, Fortressa Medicea, atop Arezzo, repairing instead to the video parlor with a pool table where the child clears the table in an inspired display of rapid fire left handed (the only thing he does left handed . . . why?) shooting, knocking in as many balls by chance as by design. The local teens stand aside and watch.

♣

The day starts later and ends later in Venice. At 9:30 AM in June it's still as fragrant and cool as it is at 9:30 PM. It's still light enough to gaze out, as far as your sight can reach, over the Guidecca, and watch turbulent waves chop at the resilient docks. Before sleep, sleepy-eyed and yawning, the child reads aloud from *Treasure Island;* then asks, yawning, "did you ever call me "L.G." (little guy) "No," Madelaine answers, "but Daddy did." I can't anymore . . . when my nine year old son is one inch shy of Keats' full height. He wakes with his arm

60

swollen from mosquito bites. "Or a spider," Madelaine suggests, pulling back his bed to look for cracks in the wall.

♣

It's not that you're encircled by water; it's more that everything is swirling, like Tintoretto in his quest to capture everything at one time in defiance of space and time.

Perspective? Venice is the place. Street names resist. Palaces and piazzas collapse into one another. The harbor shape-shifts in the mist. Nowhere is it easier to get lost. My attention is enticed, incited, to circle, to keep roving, if not like the water itself around the fixed points of the quays, then like the palaces on the Grand Canal, the gondolas, taxis, vaporettos, police boats, wherries top-heavy with mounds of cement and crisscrossed planks, and other water-bound vehicles, that swirl like brush strokes in action across the canals and wider reaches of the Adriatic.

Siena, an homage to stasis; Venice an homage to kinesis. That is why Tintoretto and Turner and Carpaccio are its truest masters and not the—however brilliant and accurate—Canaletto and Gaudi. Swollen with the remnants of ancient enthusiasms, Venice offers distraction that is not without soul. Everything that happens in Venice happens more than once. This doubling forces you to notice the slight changes that occur moment to moment, and enforces this with noises that, thanks to the acoustic richness of the place, could originate out on the water or in a bar, like this clatter of plates, the clank of spoon against cup in the (perfectly Italian) "India Cafe."

2

Siena can turn your head around too.

Maybe you lose perspective when looking at paintings without perspective. I have fallen into reveries over the golden ovals over heads in Giovanni Di Paolo's radiant canvases, but now they plunge me back into meditations about the living and the dead, the past-present . . . : experience.

Such as?

—The vacancy I felt on vacation with my father.

Or, that Sunday afternoon at poolside at the hotel Il Giardino when I watched a crowd of locals somewhere in their twenties get a little tipsy and loud and start throwing each other in the pool and I knew again that sinking "left out" feeling that I used to have in school—paralyzed in groups, tense and self-conscious, invisible to others. I found it vaguely consoling to think of Pavese's stories of his isolation among others, of watching while his friends indulged in shallow horseplay, appearing to be having fun while disguising their real feelings of terror and dismay and insecurity; then suddenly loneliness washed over me and I hoped that Sam, with no one his own age in sight to play

<h3 style="text-align:center">"Marco!"</h3>
<h3 style="text-align:center">"Polo!"</h3>

found comfort pretending to be shot, devising a new way to die each time he flopped into the water.

There are few children in Siena. I haven't actually seen any children but I assume there must be some.

It must be hard to have no time alone, or alone together.

All the more precious and intense, our fifteen minute . . . "sessions": once when he stayed at the pool while Madelaine went up to the room to get something and I went up to see what was "taking her so long"; another time in Milan when we said "why don't you go have a Seven Up at the bar and chat with the bartender, and watch that television with its big screen" . . . (amazing how quickly you can come with that kind of metaphorical gun at the head, the impending, booming, impatient, knock on the door). . . .

3

(Outnumbered)

A mere quarter mile outside Siena's walls our room at the hotel Il
Giardino buzzed and swarmed with hesitation. The morning, squan-
dered in indecision. The clouds, massing over the sky-spearing Torre
del Mangia, finally broke open. Rain pelted the maple leaves,
knocked out the poppies. It bursts in on the Anglo-Indian detective
and the blond American journalist as they get between the sheets at
last, and afterward she walks onto the viewless terrace of her Bombay
high rise wearing his—diaphanous when wet—shirt to get closer to
the monsoon's spray.

Why not admit you love the rain?
It means being only to be.

She laughed when the thunder cracked. It just burst out.

I wish they'd exchange the poolside bar
for a thunder and rain machine to break
the midday's invisible manacles, oblivion's
revenge: vapid, insidious, complete.

When you're caught in unremitting rain
with a woman and her body becomes
transparent under her light-weight and light-
colored cotton blouse and multi-purpose
skirt, the way she ultimately reacts
reveals so much about who she really is—

If we'd entered the city gates in spite of the downpour and tramped
up the crowded corridors huddled under one borrowed umbrella, we
      would have been soaked
beyond recognition and would not have heard the wind
howl through the jalousies while the child—
lost and found in his own vision—
drew the tower horizontally
to fit the dimensions of his sketch.

The raindrops came in battalions, like lances and arrows released by the Sienese army.

And the thrushes went on warbling even as they swooped toward square holes—designed for other purposes—where they might comfortably take shelter.

EVENING ON THE ZATTERE

There's a courtesan, out of Carpaccio. A masked reveler, out of
 Tiepolo.

There's Canaletto setting up his easel on the Grand Canal.

And Gaudi, another copyist.

It's true, I'm biased toward Tintoretto, his turbulence and agitation:
in "The Slaughter of the Innocents" panel at the Scuola San Rocco,
he shows a soldier hurling a baby with murderous force from the right
foreground toward the center—and yet the baby's white swaddling is
painted lightly as white gauze.

I heard he was relentless in his quest
to wrest commissions away from Titian.

Titian was the first choice for everyone
who wanted to be shown in the best light.

Tintoretto was a greedy schlemiel;
indiscriminate. And he lacked the skill
to make his objects and figures look real.

He had to struggle like hell to survive.

He would have painted the gondolas.

But whatever he painted, he made his own.

No one could deny that! And no century
has valued chaos and confusion
more than this one.

I wanted to laugh when I read in the Blue Guide for wanderers that
Tintoretto's work expressed an "inner anxiety"; there's something
comical about that kind of psychology, when applied to an artist,

however self-evident or correct, being expressed in such a pat manner, all the more humorous for being so true.

Venice, a labyrinth of alleys. Palaces out of oriental tales. Everything swirls: skirts, parasols, the water in carafes, in canals, the bodies of the walkers who do not feel their own weight, the air in the baths and temples the gods have abandoned; the robes and draperies shimmering on his canvases.

Here is where I wish you were more adept at cabala. Numerology. You found your way to section five, the number's going to become increasingly significant, you enter fifty lines, and with the door wide open and the secret, the cusp of the enigma staring at you face to face, you're blinded.

(I note you only take off those dark sunglasses when it's dark indoors, or before the screen in a dark theater . . .).

Many have come to a bad end playing with numbers.

Sunset on the Zattere. Blaze of blue tile plaque marking the hotel where John Ruskin lived overlooking the Giudecca Canal. My mind wandered to the bizarre preponderance of naked breasts in Italian magazines, still a no no in America. Sam waved at a passing yachtsman. Madelaine sat, graceful, erect and still, taking in the majestic passage of the night, the slap of the waves roused to action by the passing motorboats. A group of teenage boys ran down to the dock where some poles were tied to stakes and lines let out to catch . . . monkfish? The skinny one stripped down to his blue polka-dotted bikini underpants and dove in. And climbed out. And walked up the steps adjacent to Ruskin's house where we were resting, hopped a guard-rail, dove in, surfaced, and swam to shore, showing no awareness of the danger. (I guess he hadn't heard about the eye-infection—which never healed—that Kate Hepburn contracted doing her own stunts in *Summertime.*) Less than two centuries ago Byron could swim endlessly in these waters—turning out cantos of *Don Juan* at night on gin—and die of something more romantic than an infection accidentally contracted.

You mention breasts.

Just so.

*And you mentioned Pavese's name without mentioning the terrific power
of the scene in one of his early stories when a woman bares her breasts for
an artist. It still has the power to shock even if its contents are unremark-
able in themselves by today's jaded, world-weary, "nudity is old hat" stan-
dards. I'm talking about a violence and lust that polish, sophistication,
even over-exposure to the flesh, cannot cover up. I'm talking about . . .
surprise . . . being taken . . . unaware, like the time you saw the young
woman you had known casually and "thought" attractive—but didn't
think of too much—until you saw her running around the indoor track
in her black tights and tee shirt, sweating, pushing her body to the limit
yet remaining graceful and*

it's true, sexy beyond the limits I had set for myself that day. I wasn't
prepared to see her or be aroused and by the third time she passed I
felt, you're right, a surge . . . that in my experience only happens when
I'm surprised.

It hasn't happened to me that many times.

It can turn you into a voyeur, no?

Love at Last Sight

Years in the same apartment and never
any action in neighboring windows.
But tonight that has all changed: two stories
below, a couple has begun, under
direct light from a standing lamp; lying
side by side they touch each other's faces
tenderly, gently—he feels the down
on her cheek; puts his tongue in her mouth
and rolls his thigh between her legs as
her hips bend her pelvis arches hard

and he is kissing or biting her softly
behind her ear; they've got a rhythm going now,
even with their clothes on.

It's the best hour. If it weren't dark,
the lamp would not be shining in their room and I would not
have caught her head twisting, her hair falling
across her eyes as she rocked and he reached
under her maroon turtleneck and his hand crept
upwards and she gradually became very still.
I hoped they hadn't stopped because they saw
me at the window: how could I explain my shock
at seeing them and not the vocal coach
in the always well-lit adjacent apartment
put another diva through her paces.

I'd gone to make sure the radiator
was on (it wasn't) when the light
flooding their window caught
my attention . . . and I couldn't look away.
I was in touch with both their heartbeats now.
As she crawled over him, stealthily,
she placed her buttocks on his hips
and gripped. Getting settled
was the most electric part of her dance.
She pulsed in hypnotic cadences,
tensing her buttocks and releasing them,
swooping down to kiss his neck,
whipping her hair across his face . . . —

I liked the way she would pause,
collect herself and pull back
the chaos of her hair with both hands
while his pelvis edged her slightly upward
at the thighs. She taunted him
deliciously, tirelessly.
I didn't care if I could not see
the aureoles around her nipples.
I liked the way she leaned forward at the hips
and swept her hair across his lips and eyes.

FROM WHAT ANGLE

There are many mornings when life seems to be beginning again: limitless hope until noon, ecstasy until hunger brings you down and back.

A nun in a white habit approaches, carrying, as carefully as you would pails of well water on a rocky island in a drought, a black valise and a shopping bag marked **Nicotine.**

Why do you sit at a cafe without a view of the water, except to mark the procession of men pushing strollers, girls in short skirts running through alleys with liters of warm peach tea, a tabby cat who rubs his back against the bark and the wrens who like to light below the cafe's lush, luxurious, canopy of leaves?

Because one *doppio macchiato* costs twice as much with a view of the oily green water, glazed with dust, and I need two doubles to unsteady my nerves for the day's labors, like going into the ghetto and taking the vaporetto to Torcello, I remain happily here,
here,

listening to the Venetians greet each other this hazy summer morning while I wait to see what salve, what balm, what protection Madelaine has found to cool and quell the riot of Sam's insect bites.

Aren't you violently allergic to the pollen
that falls on your saucer?

Violently, yes faith violently. It is a real allergy, let me tell you, but dormant for the moment.

—perhaps the blessed wind, moving off the water into the city proper . . . ?

Yes. Or something else.

The boy's Byronic dive . . .

A revival of interest in the ordinary, like the taste of the vaporous foam on the coffee, or the smell of oranges.

And what brought to mind the journals with the bare-breasted women on the cover?

You can't escape. And these aren't men's magazines, sealed in plastic; they're gossip sheets like *People* or *Us* and all there is to thumb through in hotel lobbies;

or at a cafe on the diesel highway below Montereggione where we pass hours waiting for the bus, drinking *macchiato* and pondering what the message is in the way women are addressed and portrayed in Italy today, like this juxtaposition of two blond American film stars from different eras, all to make this point: "Marilyn didn't care about cellulite and Sharon Stone has none."

But the bus did come and you waved good-bye to the city ringed with towers and returned to Siena where you could wear out the soles of your sneakers walking home over the cobblestones.

Why travel if not to be apprenticed again to waiting—for bus, train, cab, plane, moment alone, food to arrive?

Waiting is an impasse it's dangerous to bypass.

But here is what our hotel manager said when we came back after having a weird experience at a restaurant in which waiting was factored out: "I have never been there, but I know they cook in the morning." I couldn't let this rest. I was enticed by the subtlety of this put-down and its usefulness as a divider, as a way of saying "this place is good because" and "this place isn't because" with a stress that goes beyond opinion, beyond subjectivity, the trivial issue of whether or not someone might have had a wonderful meal there. I liked it that the hotel manager responded to our complaints about the diminutive deep-voiced dervish of a waitress, who essentially set the steaming plates down on the table before we ordered them, literally seconds after we may have asked her what the sauce was like for a certain pasta dish. It was in its way equivalent to having your purse or shoulder bag snipped off with a razor by a roving gang of kids working together on a crowded bus in Rome: if you're unprepared, if you're not in that self-protective mode, you'll react too late because it's happening too fast for you to feel.

In the weeks prior to our arrival in Venice we had spent many hours waiting for courses to arrive. Not once had anyone flung food on our table at anything like what could be called speed. When I entered the restaurant nearest our hotel—the one Sam had impulsively burst into after a day of travel—I peeked into the kitchen where a blue flame burned steadily on the stove and a good half-dozen monkfish were crowded onto a flat round grill. I was also having a hunger fit and the monkfish, sleek gray against black iron, looked delicious—even if it had been cooked that morning and was only simmering on the grill. The hotel manager subverted me with his response because I was about to say that the restaurant made for an interesting dilemma: the food is quite good, reasonably priced—and there are times when you want to get in and out fast, as when you have plans for the evening that go beyond the evening meal . . . —but the waitress is an absolute horror, unquestionably a lunatic. I must have said something to encourage the hotel manager to say something more than that *he would never step foot in the place* even though it's a stone's throw from where he lives and quite moderate, because, he added, it was run by a family, and that with all the in-laws it was entirely possible that this mad crone had crept in and kept her job because she was family and this was . . . Venice.

This is not exactly the way my highly intelligent and superbly educated first cousin treated my highly intelligent and not superbly educated father when he took over the business his mother, unbeknownst to anyone else, owned and my father merely "ran" for fifteen years after her husband died. And my father was not a lunatic. He never willfully tried to hurt me, but when "under the influence" or possessed by his sadistic component he said things you'd find hard to believe a father would say to a son. This was a father who was angry that he had been denied his wife and son, a man who felt maligned and unappreciated. OK, so he kept me waiting for an hour or two when I, as instructed, picked him up at the office and he was still busy doing business, talking, that is, into his Dictaphone. Let's flip to the good part. He's finally ready to go, flashes the movie section of the *Times* in front of my face for a half-second and says "come on, there's

71

a new action picture that got a good review today," and in no time at all father and son were in an air-cooled heaven just off Times Square, ringed by gilded cherubim, watching *Dr. No* on the day of its release. Afterwards he would refer to me as "Mr. No," not because I always said "no," but because he found me fussy, not about external things, like food, but because of my state-of-being. He told me many times that I shouldn't worry about being drafted because they'd "never let someone like you into the army," at which point I would feel only a mild paralysis (insecure, inadequate, confused) before I came back with "why not?" Answer: "Simple. They don't want someone in the army who's always wondering if he's got something in his eye." "What?" "You know what I mean, the way you're always fiddling with your glasses." "I guess so." "You guess so. They don't want a psychoneurotic—OK, if I have to spell it out for you—who wastes valuable time worrying if he's got something in his eye." "My eye?" He found nothing more exasperating that my questioning his judgments, which he regarded as statements of self-evident facts. "DO I HAVE TO SPELL IT OUT FOR YOU? YOU'RE AN EMOTIONAL DWARF, OK? IF IT'S NOT YOUR EYE IT'S SOMETHING ELSE, OK. NOW DO YOU GET IT." (You can fill in his response when I told him I was thinking about getting contact lenses.) I was really at a loss as to my father's motive in pressing these kinds of points. I found the points themselves so peculiar that it was difficult to respond much except to maybe mutter "oh you're off the wall about all this." It never would have occurred to me to use in my defense a word he never used with regard to me: sensitive. Hypersensitive in a psychoneurotic way he would eagerly grant, but never, even as a balm to the pain he was causing me with his harsh "reality oriented" bluntness . . . sensitive.

THE DESERT OF EMPIRE

How easily our lives could have been easier if our
fathers hadn't done in whoever stood in their way.
Did progress demand they set factories belching smoke
like volcanoes? You're right to be dumbfounded as to why

you're forced to spend your time making up for
your ancestors' mistakes, waste this beautiful day
restoring ruined shrines and temples
so that the gods might not abandon Rome for good.

There could be a turn about: after they were rid of
the Etruscans, a few farsighted countrymen
had the savvy to steal their fine
sarcophagi designs, along with the booty.

Decadence is your legacy. I hold out hope
for satires, epigrams, and odes, but heaping on
the gore is not an answer, and our plays are weak
echoes of the Greeks.

If you want to have some say in the way things are,
put yourself in the hands of a higher order.
Have faith in faith. Bow down to the gods
who oversee and underwrite and sponsor.

There's nothing empirical left to this empire now.
What would have been routine raids on small fry
republics—from Vietnam to the Isle of Man—
are beaten back, and the opposition,

in ecstatic mockery, turn our spoils
to souvenir necklaces and key chains.
The ancient city, riven by civil strife,
escaped destruction by fanatic Bosnia and Iraq

with their demonic submarines, bombers,
and other dangerous toys, by a hairsbreadth.
Self-absorbed, promiscuous,
we've brought these evils on ourselves

like people who, anticipating the worst
from a routine physical, forswear
doctors until their symptoms call for
drastic measures; as only after

the condom-clogged, gaseous,
syringe-rich, toxic river
overflows and floods the litter-free,
segregated streets of the capital

will the Rivers Network organize
a mass cleanup on Earth Day.
The young, lured always by the glitter of cities,
find nothing cooler than the hotter-

than-ever-before dance-crazes flown in
from the clubs of Rio, Barcelona, or Berlin.
How was a girl to know that marriage sucks
the sap out of sex? And why not make it

with the guests, especially if it's just the boost
his mercurial career needs to rocket off . . .
How are they to know the sexual spectacles
began on their own ravaged ground?

And these out-of-towners are so endlessly grateful
for a dose of decadence because they
"sure don't get pussy like this in Topeka."
(The New Age victor is the one who gets

the onlooker to come without anything
physical happening between them.)
"How does he think I know how to get the dry-
cleaning-mogul's cock to stiffen, as if a good

dis weren't hard to find, like 'you use your tongue
like you're trying to remove a spot.'"
Her husband, in his white tux, appeared
nonchalant, but a second glance revealed

a man slaphappy and dazed from one
too many Zombies; either way,
when the *Titania II* pulls into port
she'll allow whoever has the best

offer, captain or mutineer, Delano or
Benito Cereno, to take her on the dance floor.
Dalliance supplies what she needs for her shopping sprees
which "this guy whose wedding ring I like never

take off can't get through his head are
necessary. He's so dense, like I show up
in this designer dress on my 'allowance.'
Men have no idea what it costs a girl to be

truly glamorous in times like these—
and when they land the commission
remain clueless as to why they
were chosen and not the other guy

with the goody-two-shoes type wife."
It's shattering to consider that these nerds,
for whom watching's the real
turn on, sprang from fierce, sturdy stock

who in their youth conquered conquerors,
brought down swaggering, gallant
Hannibal, Pyrrhus, and Antiochus,
dyeing the sea red with Punic blood.

But the early Romans, the soldier-farmers,
knew better than to double think what had to be done,
and dug with the tools of the long-gone Sabines,
and never neglected to cut the logs to honor

mom's firm yet anxious request for firewood as
shadows shifted on a far rise, night
fell, and man and oxen were the same
in their deep desire to lie down.

Who is immune from ruin by time?
Each generation wearier than the one before;
these days no one deigns to have children
until they are "professionally secure."

And the media waits long and long to warn
the idealists born during the baby-boom
that the future is also being sabotaged:
undone by sluggish sperm; hardened wombs.

(after Horace, Odes, Book III, 6)

"NOT NORMALISSIMO"

I

He tore you down and aggrandized the blind deaf and dumb.

A masterful sadist.

You were in New York again over one school holiday or another.

It was warm and humid, I remember people mopping their brows with immense handkerchiefs, the mirror shimmer of the silver ice bucket, the relief of the air-conditioning

and found yourself at a party surrounded by two unfamiliar familiars, the two deaf men: your cousin Heschel Levy and his pal Isaac Lark. They were both wildly friendly toward you, animated and gesticulating. Then the slender, quiet, saint-like, blind Wilhelm Lark appeared at the edge of the circle. He no sooner touched your hand than he said, (quietly), "Mark."

I liked the way my harsh name sounded on his lips. He quieted the consonant.

"How could you tell it was me?"
"I can tell."
"But I haven't seen you for a few years . . ." at what must have been a gathering of the Lark clan.

Wilhelm smiled. He had heard skeptical pagans like myself resist the powers of touch before and he would, as before, listen and endure. He would be patient.

This was like a rite in which whatever innate goodness you had was confirmed, underscored, by the blessing implicit in the attentions of these three handicapped men.

Isaac Lark: salt and pepper hair, tall, dapper, blue blazer, blue striped shirt, gray pleated slacks, red and blue bow tie. Magnetic.

You describe him as if a deaf man shouldn't be able to dress himself, when the blind boy, only a few decisive years older than you but "ageless in his wisdom," according to your Dad,

was the one who might have had a problem *but settled on a uniform,* white shirt, blue blazer, gray wool slacks, subdued tie.

Your father got wind of your presence at the party.

"I heard about it all," he said.
"About what?"
"Everything. I got the lowdown."
"From whom?"
"I have informants. But I can assure you that Wilhelm Lark thinks very highly of you."
"I like him too."
"What's not to like?"

I pretended not to hear his barbed question and continued. "Was he born blind? Or did he become blind? How does he live? Does he live with someone?"
"What do you think?"

And then my father couldn't resist saying, in the hushed tones he reserved for those who were truly great: "Have you ever heard him play the piano?"

Anyone who could play an instrument was tops in my father's book. His second wife would replicate his sacred murmur when she would draw me aside and tell of how overcome she was when my father played the organ for her once before they were married. Why wouldn't he consent to play the organ for me? Just once. "Your father doesn't like showing off. He's a deeply humble man." Remarks like this always sent my mind spinning. Why couldn't he do it just to do it?

I had endured enough hours with that silent organ brooding in the alcove of the spacious, gloomy rent-controlled apartment with its tenacious splash of blood on the rug that hung on long after his encounter with the edge of a new glass coffee table. He and my mother had lived there during the year they were together. He had stayed on alone in the fifteen years between my mother's departure and his second wife's insistence that she would marry him but only if they moved. "Come on Dad," (how awkward it was for me to call him that! How less plangent than "Daddy Sidney"!) "I'd love to hear you play," and he would look at me as if I were both mad and impudent: how could someone as "musically illiterate" as myself possibly appreciate the quality of his playing, to say nothing of a sonata by Brahms, whose melodious line he favored (and hummed, perhaps unaware that he was doing so). I never doubted he could play the organ, or at the very least perform a few pieces on the organ, but I didn't find that possibility tantalizing enough to work at breaking down his resistance. I asked him several times, nicely, and when he answered "never mind," I didn't ask any more.

Even in my youth I could instantly translate the double message he was sending (with telepathy worthy of a Dr. Mabuse) with this reference to Wilhelm's skill on the piano: (a) a blind man can do what you, with the use of your two eyes, can't do; (b) you'll never be able to appreciate me because you haven't the training to evaluate my musical talents.

I didn't buy into his shtick, but I was utterly at a loss as to why he invested so much energy into making himself appear to be such a mystery, like a hidden treasure it was my job to unearth, making it so "abundantly clear," to borrow one of the phrases he ran into the ground, that I was such a pathetic *dumbkopf,* barely worth the effort he put in to "try and explain things" to me. (Whenever I asked "why" he'd roll his eyes and answer, gruffly, "*Why?* If you don't get it I can't help you." Then he'd mutter "why, why" two or three more times and shake his head. Then a "no, I take it back. You'll find out why. Someday. Someday you'll be possessed [his word!] to get to know me, to find out who I really am, you'll see.") But then his contempt for "the hicktowns," where I had lived with Mom and the itinerant Rabbi, the outposts I embraced as we moved further west across America, was limitless: like his anger that, in the end, swallowed him up; like the sea on whose surface he spent every possible waking hour during his bleak end, his headlong plunge from the terrace into the parking lot—the implosion that was the last ten years of his life.

You're sure . . . ?

I'm not sure, but it popped out and I don't want to waffle: it sounds right. Even if it isn't *logical.*

Interesting. (Sound of someone drawing on a pipe.) He had contempt and you were afflicted with a passion to return, if not to the "hicktown" itself, to a town that could have been its . . . double.

2

Close to the Ground

Lost in a northern suburb of Chicago, I turned
onto a street that runs parallel to the lake then
meanders toward bluffs where roses surround
a shagbark hickory and gorged crows
strain the branches. After some whiffs of lilac
and after admiring the climbing vines, sparse
but tenacious, on the cathedral brick of the houses,
I could just glimpse, through the sinuously

arching elms—whose topmost leaves sparked
when they touched—a trace of blue and the lisp
of water on the shore, where white
boutiqued rocks, moss and mica-free,
formed jetties to keep the waveless waves
in tow; leaving so much light
dead alewives glittered as they fouled the air,

and the muskee's many pointed teeth
flared inside its crushed jaw.
After a break on the airbrushed cemetery lawn
behind gravestones that blocked the lake-wind,
I stalked shadows, quickened my stride
along the mazy paths and detours and passed
off-white-leaning-toward-gray one-story
wooden houses, benches creaking on
screened-in porches, geraniums in pots,

cats blinking at eye-level, *plein air*
sketches of maples, the puppet-dance
of their shadows on the house-fronts,
the hordes of underrated dandelions whose heads—
once I abandoned the meticulous trowel—

I swatted off gleefully with my baseball bat. . . .
They were still there: the bicycles turned over in the yards,
their spokes interlaced like lovers' limbs
preserved in the Vesuvian lava-flow that leveled Naples,
the girls playing with blocks in their driveway,
the mothers, alone, dragging the long cords of their telephones
through the glare of kitchen steel and porcelain,
desparate to get somebody on the line;
and but for the cries of the construction crew
blasting debris out of the gutters with an air gun,
and to the south the prairie burning . . . ,
this was my childhood—"shot"—on another location. . . .

There are paths in the fog, even in the dark,
and they fork, even in the light.

3

It gnaws that I can't remember what I was doing in New York, how
old I was, or why I had gone to the party in the first place. It may have
been a party of the deaf . . . or a Lark family gathering. And it was
startling to see my cousin Heschel on my mother's side of the family
in the room with so many of my father's friends. I'm guessing that the
party was at Isaac Lark's apartment so that his family (including the
blind Wilhelm) and many of his deaf friends were invited.

I was in love with one branch of the Lark family, none of whom were
there, or appeared too late for it to matter, and consisted of my
father's best friend, his wife, son and daughter. The children were
older than me, more or less finishing high school as I was beginning.
The son, Joshua, was so kind to me during the summer weeks when I
stayed with them that he went so far as to take me along on dates with
him so that I shouldn't get lonely, only he once made the mistake of

asking if it was safe for him to back up in a crowded lot and I said "yes," dreamily, without really looking closely, the word came involuntarily to my lips, and the subsequent crunch of his parents' finned white Chrysler with spaceship interior against the fender and headlights of a Ford Galaxie ruined my credibility with him. He'd only had his license for a year or so and was still allowed to use the car on a trial basis. He told the story of how he asked me if it was all right to back up whenever he could forever after.

From then on he treated me with the same affection but a certain suspicion. And indulged in lighthearted teasing, "and don't forget to get Mark to tell you if it's all right to back up," he'd yell to my father. While I reveled in their attention and affectionate teasing, it irritated me a little that they frequently exchanged glances, winks, and little smiles, when I told them some anecdote about Life With Mother and the "Rabbi" in the West and seemed to take much of what I had to say as if it were a sign, or symptom, of my state of mental unwellness. And Josh would introduce me to one of his friends and say "Mark wanders around Chicago alone with his other ten year old friends, who carry knives and brass knuckles. They're tough kids, right Mark?" It wasn't that my criminal life was out of his imaginative range, it was more that the families in their close-knit orthodox community sent their children to nurturing private schools. I envied their protected life.

(Joshua was forced to revise his opinion as to who I really was over and over again. One time he was driving through Massachusetts where I'd been sent to a summer school near Great Barrington that turned out to be more like reform school. My typically "wild stories" about the place had filtered down to him, and he got out of the car half-smirking in anticipation of the contrast between my reports and what he would encounter. "I hear this is quite a place: where are all the juvenile delinquents?" I thought a quick tour of the dorm was in order. Between the smell of airplane glue, the slicked back hair and tattoos on the biceps of the greasers lifting weights, he could see I was in reality fighting to survive. When we walked back to his car, he wondered aloud, chastened and amazed, "how could your father have sent you to such a place.")

$$\clubsuit$$

His mother Joanne and I were really close: we shared an antic repartee in each other's company. If I questioned how she could talk so fast while dishing out pancakes with a cigarette in her mouth without dropping ashes into the food, she'd talk even faster: "you mean like this? Markdoesn'tundertsandhowIcantalksofastwithacigaretteinmymouthandservethefoodwithoutgettingashesinit." It got to where when we saw each other she'd start with how "Markdoesn'tunderstand . . ." and we'd both become hysterical with laughter while the others assumed a mask of mild tolerance.

♣

The Lark daughter, Felicia, was rarely around, and there was a lot of talk of how she had developed into a "real woman," how beautiful she had become, so when she appeared for a few days while I was staying with them on the Jersey shore I was curious to witness this fabled transformation from girl to young woman.

My father joined us on the weekends.
Clearing his throat, to speak
with statesman-like sobriety,
informed me that Felicia had cast off the [diminutive]
nickname by which I had known her
all my life. I protested: why couldn't
we call her CiCi and her new friends
call her Felicia? Charles'
contempt rolled off me—I would present
my question to my pal Joanne: "Felicia
is a lovely name, but would she mind if . . . ,
since I've always been a kid to her . . . ,
I still called her CiCi?"

"Probably not. It's not your
image of her she's trying to change.
Sometimes parents, especially fathers,
and older brothers have a very
hard time dealing
with their little darlings becoming women . . ."

"Why?"

83

"How old are you anyway now Marko?"

"Almost 11."

"It's common for fathers and daughters to form
a powerful bond; but they aren't always fully aware . . .
and the bond is more powerful than
the conscious mind can fully grasp."

"Frederick doesn't want CiCi to go on dates!"

"She's still his . . . little girl . . . no
matter how permissive he pretends to be."

"Is it the same with you and Josh?"

"I hope not. I don't think so."

"I can't believe that Josh lets me come along
on his dates. I wish he were my brother."

(She pops a cigarette in her mouth.)

"He does too. He thinks you're very deep for your age."

"I'm so happy here. It's the first
time I ever felt what it was like
to be part of a   fam . . . ily."

"You mean you don't like being passed
back and forth and back and forth,
east and west?
It would drive anyone crazy!"

Study for Male Gaze

She was just seventeen and I, say twelve,
when she entered the red room and sat down

84

facing me on the wing chair in the center.
Her mother said: "I'm going to have to teach you how
to cross your legs in a tight skirt."
I shivered for her humiliation.
Wanted to see what I'd missed, but what?
Then without lowering my head, gazed down.
Was there more than the juncture where
girdle and stocking interlocked,
or the nylon rustling when she dragged
one thigh across the other?

I didn't feel a whit guilty that I happened to be
at the kitchen window of the beach house
when this same girl, back from baking
on the sand in the midday heat,
stepped under the outdoor shower
and peeled off her fulsome,
unrevealing, one-piece suit

to wash the sand off her breasts . . . :
her matter-of-fact quickness
couldn't stop the slow, cold water
from caressing each strand of her
long thick brown hair, through which, later,
after she'd rung it out like a mop,
she would drag a wide-toothed comb.
What was time? Flames escaped the crown
of my head, my heart raced in fear
that she'd catch me staring, as if I had lain in wait.

Then, in the ritual way of women,
she did the other, modest, maddening thing:
wrapped her torso in a towel.

♣

I will tell you simply why I stayed so long engaged. The two deaf men
paid intense attention to me, and they took a long time and great
pleasure in explaining how they knew each other. And then, deploy-
ing another strategy to keep me listening, tactlessly asked if I knew

"your mother used to go out with Gerald Lark?" And "did you know that the Larks got your mother and father together in the first place?"

The nefarious Gerald, who to her immense disbelief, tried to feel her up on their first date, before she "smacked him good?"

"I didn't know that," I lied, feigning surprise and refraining from correcting their revisionist history.

They dragged me over to see Gerald, who was holding court around the spread, trying to talk and chew a bagel with the same mouth. His lips were smeared with cream cheese. It was like clown makeup that he couldn't remove with broad, bold strokes of the napkin; without looking in the mirror. The deaf and blind were dressed so elegantly, why was Gerald so altogether linty and wrinkled, why did the cuffs of his pants drag along the carpet? I had always been fascinated by his pockmarked face. The other Larks had jet-black hair and smooth faces and favored black suits. Why had this curse, this grayness, pallor, and disfigured face, been visited on Gerald?

"The measles epidemic . . . and he couldn't resist picking. . . ."

Isaac and Heschel conspired to get Gerald's attention with a pantomime: they kept pointing at me bringing their hands to their knees and raising them above my head.

(None of us could know you reached your full height at fifteen.)

I translated as "remember the little boy you . . . once knew . . . ," and still in the end had to spell it out for this preoccupied Lark.

This was the same Gerald, who appeared old and gray even when he was some ten years younger and my father and I met up with him in Miami and he crumpled a five spot in my palm under the towering palms: an enormous sum by my standards

and so I looked forward, if not to seeing him, the ugly, less than personable Gerald, than to saying good-bye and . . . that moment when he would reach into his wallet, and I stood there, breathless with anticipation at the miraculous substances I could purchase in abundance, gum, baseball cards, *Mad,* smokes.

I would also ponder the following mystery. Why did Gerald give me more money when we said good-bye than my own

(by then blind, and he dressed himself, color coordinated, no problem)

grandfather Abraham Levy who, in crumpling a couple of singles slyly into my palm as he would a headwaiter or microfilm to an espionage agent, would also urge me not to spend it and, when I was old enough to travel around Manhattan alone, added that I should take the bus and not waste $ on expensive taxis.

I didn't see my cousin Heschel, whom my grandfather respected far more than his phlegmatic brother, (or my "slick" father or my stepfather "who had the nerve to argue" with him) until shortly before he died and the first thing he did after this twenty year hiatus was to launch into the story of the party where, did I remember?, I had talked for hours with him and Isaac. But he couldn't tell me how I got there.

The prison movie your son,

stricken with homesickness for his native city and language,

was dying to see en Inglese <Shawshank Redemption> *never arrived at the theater, and you stood in the box office staring at the byzantine schedules to secure the other possible days and times of day other American and English films would be shown in* original language, *joined by two equally desperate teenagers and one glamorous black-haired woman in a black silk dress and heels who exclaimed she was also "dying" to see it, consoled herself with ("impossible to get!") tickets for the concert at 8, and now had to decide "how to kill the next three hours."*

Antonio Vivaldi

Four Seasons

Sold Out (italian)

I'd rather watch kids eel fishing and diving
into the lagoon than fight for tickets
to hear a piece I've heard played with brio on vinyl
and—unforgettably—on celluloid
in Monuchkine's epic film
where she choreographed Moliere's
death scene to the Allegro
as he took one step and then another
up the red carpeted stairs, spitting blood
in agonizing slow motion.

But what about the spectacle itself,
the piazza in black and white,
luminous, transparent, the imaginary chandelier of the sky,
and then all around you on an earthly level,
the fireflies, fireworks, and lanterns
perched on the facades.

And the Tomahawks whistling toward Destination Bosnia, a day's
ride from Venice.

*And why did you abandon Torcello so quickly? From there you could have
seen the marshlands near the mainland, the Lido.*

In passing . . . there wasn't time.

*Maybe there was something else you chose to visit over Torcello on your
last day.*

A choice I regret, but won't lament.

There isn't much to see, but after all,
Venice was built from the stones of Torcello.
They poled barges almost too heavy to float
through the marsh and across the lagoon.

And a local boy smuggled St. Mark's
putrefying flesh out of Byzantium
by hiding it under a load of fresh pork
to get it past the customs inspector.

And now you can't escape the shadow of the Campanile
named after him and, sequestered in the shadows,
the five-headed shell of the Cathedral.

Did you go to the ghetto?

I knew you'd ask. I can hear you asking.

I just asked if you went.

I resented the idea of a guide.

But the danger of defacement!

They seemed to time the time when they would
point to the gilded six-pointed stars.

So it wasn't a rote recitation . . .

I fought back tears. These visits to the old
and abandoned synagogues set my thoughts
on a downward course.

I like that "downward course." You think I don't weep . . .

When I asked the guide if the much maligned, misunderstood and
therefore *almost Jewish* Tintoretto lived in the ghetto he

> barked out   absolutely   not
> while several blocks from the interior a sign
> for the Hotel Tintoretto reared up
> (while bells clanged antiphonally across the city)
> and I stopped in to ask the question:
> Did He live around here?

"Oh yes, there's a plaque somewhere on the next street . . ."

*So: not strictly in the ghetto but more or less in the Jewish quarter.
Because as the odd man out, whose work was sometimes applauded and
sometimes reviled—criticized for haste . . .*

the loose white lines he drew to outline figures,
to illuminate where there was no light
in the dusky chapels

*fought like a demon for commissions and perfection to him was the oppo-
site of, say Veronese's. . . .*

Only 25 Jewish families remain in Venice proper; 50 if you count the
outskirts. The families who escaped during the Holocaust never came
back: they didn't want to live in a place where such things can hap-
pen.

And yet that night along the canal I forgot about it all, even the lousy
squid in its own ink

you never tired of trying, the polenta deserved to be called

—don't say it!—

and I was swept away by the lights streaking the black water and the
light wind lifting the sheets like sails in the rooms above the canal

> and I thought of Moroni's bronze
> horseman who lives
> outside the Peggy Guggenheim museum
> with an erection that will never die down,
> arms and legs outstretched
> in a wide V,
> riding on, however still he might appear
> to the naked

> eye—that registers only
> the husk, the shell, the semblance;

> the cellulite instead of the soul.

Yet sometime in the eighteenth century
the Jews broke down and hired a Christian
sculptor to renew the temple.

I can neither defend nor condemn, and
since the Jews still weren't allowed to be
artists in Venice, it's hard to form a—

*No, **merchants**, remember?*

Fewer and fewer Venetians every year.
The palazzos all turned into hotels. All this beautiful
eccentricity on the decline.

The prophets are scathing in their
castigation of the people.

It can be rousing to be upbraided.

Don't get kinky on me.

Everything done without reconsidering
the root of the reason becomes tiresome.

The prophets' excoriations
kept the Jews
from becoming jaded, self-satisfied.

Is that "the power of the Schwartz"?

Soon the Venetians and the Jews will share this:
they'll be plaqued to death.

Because I do not
belong to a congregation doesn't
mean I don't embrace the Judaic ethics . . .

Are you asking for pity. Or future
sky miles for not rejecting the entire
value system I tried to pass over
"with love, from me to you?"

Do you take me for a scoundrel, sir?

You know I don't and I know you're trying
to provoke and trick the little Rabbi.
I can smell the bait in those fetid canals.
But can you sense that what you gain being
a heathen is like gambling against
the odds in Vegas or Monte Carlo,
exchanging the surety of glitter now
for what the cabalist knows:
that if you delete one and substitute another—

the shallow future's gesture to appease
the vanquished . . .

that heathen's seven letters are a
clue . . . and all you have to do is delete
the "th" the black magicians slipped in
for the "v" that was there initially
and you've restored the word and letter:

heaven, victory, and the feminine,
part,
where all dreams and desires begin.

The Heavens

The heavens let you return to earth one
day every seven years. How am I so sure
they aren't decades, scores, or more? Answer:
there isn't an extant god who isn't
cognizant that life on earth has limits
that are rubbed out the instant the spirit
ascends, having conspired to escape

the body's incessant continuum.
Death always gnawing away.
Only those whom these inviolable
truths grasp hold of with their talons
can't shake themselves free from uncertainty
and the secret violence at its source
to take comfort from the bread
and wine, and sense the threshold near when
stumbling! O much maligned embarrassment!

You who compel this self-control consumed
species to scatter a few precious clues
to show: the outside is the inside,
beginning with the blush, the turning red,
and the involuntary trembling
that seer and teen can recognize at once,
and through this insight share some common ground.

♣

You refer to matters that are often
overlooked. And by raising this discourse
to a loftier height, by not keeping a too close watch over
my . . . actions . . . you were free to keep your hand on the dial
until a signal came through, and there was silence
in the temple, before you broke the spell,
and translated the code, rocking any unbelievers:
"For he is invisible, not silent!"

No progenitor or prime mover can
control what the inheritors will do,

and the quest is set in motion.
And the youngest son,
when he turns
thirteen, doesn't ask what life means.

When the family comes together
on Passover
                and his fork
falls to the floor
              he
                  lets it slide
further under the table, to see if thigh is all
his four adolescent female
cousins are offering down below
this year,
          on the night we recline,
and as the men loosen their belts

he goes under again, *now where
could it have gone* my lovely young
napkin,
        and as he hoped and dreamed,
one cousin—thinking the same thoughts?—
slipped off her panties when she'd gone
to the bathroom and he could hear
her asking, "if we 'teens' could go
and hang and listen to music,"

knowing the drowsy, recumbent grownups,
would answer "sure, the service is over,

celebrate the freedom your ancestors
wrested from the opposition. Do what
feels right, and if no one knocks at the door
it means we're sleeping over—though I doubt
your mother will want to since she didn't
bring her . . . and would have to wear the same clothes
two days in a row, while you, dear daughter,
would find a tee shirt to sleep in and I
am used to sleeping only in my skin.

But when 25 loosely related
people converge over thousands of miles,
I think we may perhaps unknowingly,
share a common necessity."

The Japanese will buy Venice—

Even a Howard Hughes or a Donald Trump couldn't just buy a city
like that. The Venetians wouldn't—

But they won't have any say. The sale will occur in Rome.

Unless they band together. And form a separate government, maybe
even a country,

as Quebec is always threatening to do from Canada.

There was a time when all 117 islands had their own vegetable garden.

Imagine the Sienese thinking: maybe we should be our own country
too.

Siena itself is a museum.

Like Venice.

More like a fortress. Even the olive rows are precise.

Like Vegas.

The beautiful falsity of the Roman statues at Caesar's Palace.

The imitations.

Grateful to see a pair of white *Nike*'s drying on a windowsill in Siena.

There's something to be said for going backward, returning to older forms of government, before the world is sold out from under us.

And you won't have to go to EuroDisney . . . —or the Warsaw that was built to the specifications of the Warsaw before the bombing.

Even the India Cafe where I roost these clement June mornings is a chain, but I don't know if it's owned by an Indian corporation or if it alludes to . . . early voyages to India . . .

Like Marco Polo and China . . . and pasta . . .

Like "Chinese Cafe." I hunger for your touch a long lonely time.

Throughout my childhood and youth I was forced to listen to stats about the "number of Jewish families" in the outposts where the little Rabbi, Rider, stepfather, had his congregations, and the towns where his colleagues held posts, and the towns where he should have gone— congregations he actually visited.

The term is interview.

What bound these Jews together was this vague sense of a necessity to band together that had very little to do with god.

Or everything . . . maybe they didn't know where it would end.

That God fills us with compulsions—and governs our actions invisibly.

96

It's like a couple who meet to have sex a few times a week, and some-times spend the night, who then discover that they like being inside each other because they like each other, only it never occurs to them to think about it that way.

TOMAHAWK

My deaf cousin had a hand in designing the Tomahawk Missile.
The blueprints open on his desk for what was to become
a show-and-tell-style reunion.

I hadn't laid eyes on this exuberant man since chance
threw us together at a party *given by his best friend*
whose brother was your real *father's best friend,*

and whose blind nephew appeared, shook my hand,
and, unprompted, said my name:—it was like a blessing.
The deaf men nodded at the blind boy's recognition.

They held me captive, these two deaf friends, and took forever
with frantic mimicry explaining how they knew each other,
firmly guiding the silent dialogue toward the bizarre

intersection of fates: theirs, mine, my father's, my mother's. . . .
The deaf find ways of contacting each other.
They have their own watering holes.

Did he place this decisive warhead above all other
constructions executed during a working life spent
gratefully, perhaps too gratefully, in the government's

employ designing, mainly, destroyers . . . ?
Final proof he was not handicapped by his handicap?
He married a deaf woman, but his two daughters

are normal; I mean not deaf. . . . Both were present
and married. One was pregnant. The other became
more and more voluble as this Sunday marathon wore on.

Conversation meant—: asking each other questions.
My cousin scribbled answers alongside the next question
on a pad that rustled like a pet hamster in his back pocket.

It was work, talking to that generation's deaf.
It was hard not to raise your voice.
I caught my mother trying to catch my eye

across the smoked fish infested spread
as she mouthed a lipsticky YOU MUST E NUN CI ATE
Brain-dead from the labor of "catching up"

with veritable strangers with whom I was linked
by blood, I wandered, coffee balanced in saucer,
toward my cousin's study, in vain hope of a tête-à-tête.

He followed, hauled down sheafs from shelves,
while I studied the framed sketches of ship's interiors.
Had deafness helped him achieve these heights of invention?

His face brightened. He strained with strangled voice to answer.
Even I could understand "That's the ticket,"
before he scrawled with *Bic* on pad. "Deaf . . . can think better. . . ."

I was about to say "Not all," that I was asking
about him personally, when his daughter intervened
and said, aloud and in sign, that this was "deafism."

He signed: "No no, not hearing forced me . . ."
She signed and spoke, indulgent, resigned, admiring:
"So deafness makes you superior?"

I liked the way she stood up to him, and the way he took it.
Trying not to sound like a boorish upstart in a Q & A
disingenuously grilling Oppenheimer, Einstein or Bohr

with how they felt about their elegant theorems
culminating in so much death, I asked if
he was ambivalent about designing warheads. Question

from left field. Bewilderment squared.
His honked "Wa" was like an inaudible "Come again?"
Forehead painfully wrinkled. Deep-set ridges.

My stomach contracted: Oh God, what have I done?
It wasn't me asking discomfiting questions to hound
this dear, sweet, ebullient man, who had done his best . . . ;

it was my . . . duty to ask, which appeared to perplex
this . . . disembodied intelligence . . . schooled in
focusing on the problem to be solved just as

Husserl bracketed words, [postponed]
this longing to belong to sentences that mimicked
meaningful action, and to block out the politics and social

contexts that could . . . derail . . . the (beautiful) concord
between pure thought and necessity. He had the right to think:
Anyone can design a ship, or a missile, that works

like a bigger bullet shot from a bigger gun;
but to invent one that can stop, turn around,
change direction, now that's—invention.

She repeated the question in sign and came back
with: "My father doesn't understand your question."
I spoke more slowly. "You must feel proud at how

the Tomahawk conducted itself during the Desert War."
The praise sent him rocking. So that's what I took so long
to say! He nodded exuberantly in accord.

"Wait. Even though it was for a good cause
doesn't it bother you that the missile
killed many people." Question from left field.

Flurry of signs between father and daughter.
"My dad says war is horrible but once you're in
it's important to win." "That was true before,

and true as it pertained to the two world wars,
but Southeast Asia . . . was another story."
Groan of dismay. Why should a deaf engineer

be forced to deal with relative ethics too . . . ? War
made the mental challenge of his work more
challenging, as it did the group holed up at Los Alamos.

The heart sinks when these higher mathematical formulations
become subject to weather, and the stray jackrabbits and *homo
 sapiens*
"who weren't supposed to be anywhere near the test site . . ."

This pacific man could not have thought about what the Tomahawk
did to real live—now dead—people.
He was too immersed in the question of how

to get the missile to think, to take into account—the wind.

ACROSS A CROWDED ROOM

Mabuse could do it.

Not sure. He could aim his bushy eyebrows and intent stare
at his opponent across the card
table, and get them to throw or not take
the card that would have meant a winning hand,
but as for getting the cocksure unwitting gambler
to rise in a trance, like one whose body
has been snatched, obtain a gun and pump five
slugs into the cop who was hounding him . . .

I don't know.

But you would agree that the Nazis did capitalize on Mabusian tactics.

Grossly, yes.

Mabuse was a class-act.

Like the spectral villains who pop up in Bond—
from Dr. No to Ernst Stavro Blofeld—

or that dude with the   nipple
        (or no   nipples
        shit—can't—remember)

And you're still baffled   not to say

tormented   *as to why
your father Charles called you "Mr. No"
when you didn't see yourself as a kid*

who reaches automatically to squeeze
        the trigger of No
whenever someone at least

three times his age,
heavier and shorter . . .

It is, I have to admit, curious.
But nobody forced you to spend time with that . . .

2

There's Mabuse and Mabuse.

And there are those who do
the Mabusian thing,
without having a clue
who they're imitating,

those who out of envy,
or jealousy, spot a rival
"across a crowded room"
and think, maybe I can make her

drop her drink and spot
her imitation mail dress
irrevocably,

red wine rolling down
her cleavage like blood— . . .
Carrie—!

—is a Mabuse—

Like that woman who fell prey
to Primal Therapy.

A year of beating
the heck out of sofa cushions;
then she flattened the padding, her fist
struck the hard wood floor,
and it was over.

And you know what.

What.

The guy who played Goldfinger, I mean the actor who played the real Goldinger in the movie . . .

yeah (who are you now?)

He played Mabuse in The Thousand Eyes of Doctor Mabuse.

Never sat through that one.

How come? I thought you were a fan of Lang's . . .

Sound. I didn't want Mabuse to talk.

Are you like this . . . —all the time?

Like what?

Hanging on words?

Gert Frobe. That's the actor's name.

Huhwhat?

Who played both Mabuse and Goldfinger.

His name came up during one of your history lessons

don't dignify a class by calling it a lesson

at Rideaway because the students, excuse my language, pronounced the great German poet's name as Gert.

Better than girth.

By a narrow margin.

The imminent death of my grandfather
lay heavy on my mind as I walked

toward—or in the general direction of—
history class . . . where the unanswered

questions would be waiting on the blackboard,
(questions I longed to replace with other

questions—to which the genial southern
gentleman who had us in his charge each

11th hour—always responded
with places, names, and dates).

It was hard to concentrate much on the past
when the light of these late autumn days

showered a cool radiance on juniper, sage, saguaro, and arroyo—
(blessed reprieve from the summer's pulverizing heat

and winter's aloof, dour absence, unnerving
in its cruel removal of color)—and on Tory Wilderness,

a fetching, free-spirited blond from Oahu
who glided across the walkways in an off yellow skirt.

The old southern gent didn't mark you absent
if you just *appeared*—before the final

        Bell . . . *brrring*

that signified—what else?—dismissal.
Chalk took advantage of its dustiness

to flee the nouns it was to designate.
Easygoing is one thing, but to let this horde of

unruly teens fling spitballs and paper airplanes . . . —
as the places, names and dates of their own

accord, "removed themselves" from the blackboard,
soared and dove, forming new and unseen

combinations just long enough for us to register
the shock of that possibility and

the attendant terror: that if nothing
in the "past" was fixed—how should we live?

If all of history was this impermanent
on what should we fix our sighs and sights?

(Don't make me bring the Warren Commission
into this . . . , not now, not here, . . .).

I heard the laughter of Herodotus, Nostradamus,

Not yet!

                                    and Vico.

No Spengler?

He was tired of being proved correct.

3

"Mr. Rudman, just sit down, and I'll mark you here."

"How do I know that what I read in here is true?"

"There are some things you have to take on faith.
I'm not asking you to verify . . . it's all in Mr. Parkman

America's greatest historian . . . and a hero in his own way:
he had so much pain in his body he had to write

in the bathtub, on a board he set across the sides.
So no excuses when it's time for term papers!"

"Yeah. But in our text book *with these stupid illustrations for babies* it doesn't say anything about witnesses.

Anonymous here just says—it happened this way—
and I just think whoever claims that this . . . Wolfe . . .

stood up in the boat with his arm tucked into his coat
like Napoleon—and recited some ode

about graves and churches the instant before a bullet
took him out, has seen too many movies."

4

This fit of brashness in the sleepy class provoked a barrage of chuckles from our genial leader. *"I can see him now, midway through the battle . . .*

It was not 'too late.'
It was worse than that:
the bullet was en route
to Wolfe's good heart.

(I have a replica of it here,
pass it around would you . . .
you couldn't fire more than once
with a musket but once you hit

your target the ball blasted away
a lot of muscle and bone,
in addition to the vital organ
if your aim was true.

I bought it in Quebec City.
Has anyone here been there?
(Raises hand to call for a raise of hands.)
Figured as much.

I'll bet you that Coach Farmington's
mustangs have wandered that far north.
Heck, maybe even that nice young
woman who began teaching French

here this fall, Madame . . . Madame . . ."
"Claire," "thank you could arrange an expedition."
Class: "An expedition?" "No of course
not I meant . . . a field trip. . . .

Look: Wolfe could have
gone in disguise or
hunkered low so no one
could get to him.

He had gone this far.
He had other lives
in his care; it was
a *Point of Honor*

and Wolfe's legacy
is that of herald to what
may yet come to pass
in terms of human

possibility. Salmon
struggle upstream,
against odds that would empty
the world's casinos.

In no-time flat!
I never learned to doubt
everything like you.
Never had that . . . luxury.

I'm not an expert
on motivation,
but history, well
I know my history.

The reasons you're prone
to what you now call
suspicions may not stem
from anything more—

—or less—than genetic
disposition.
I did. Later on.
Get interested.

In philosophy. Hell,
by the end of one dizzying year
between the *two* world wars,
we covered everything from

Aristotle to Kant.
Have you ever been fogged-in?
That's what happened to my head.
I discovered that the question mark

could be the devil incarnate.
(Writes one on the blackboard. Tries to erase it.
Asks for "a volunteer, a boy *or* a girl,"
to run to the bathroom to wet the sponge.)

Stick with history, the facts,
ladies and gentlemen, the facts.
You weren't ready for ideas.
I taught my class so the dumb-

est kids could pass and—get out of this
place they'd no desire to be in
and stay out of the war
(not that *I* was against

it but I didn't want to see you boys
die; not just yet; not before you 'gotit'
through your skulls that life
was not some stroll across

that patch of desert there.
(Silence as all stare out the window
and register the dangers.)
Not one of you was ready

to have thoughts, which
for Goethe you see, meant action.
Wolfe may rather have written
Gray's 'Elegy' than taken

Quebec, but his act is all
that counts, not the intention.
I—chose—not—to—waste your—
time— . . . on conundrums.

That reminds me.
I had the map down
to show how country
flowed into country,

when I could not *not*
let Goethe's name drop
out and follow up with a—
breezy précis of his varied life.

Then I overheard the kids yammering
during break about—*Gert*
as if two syllables were one too many
for your puny brains!

Go-ethe—I asked you
to repeat and got—
Goeth—'Hey man here's where I do
my botany.

No—don't go in there—
that's where I work on my—magnum
opus—come along—
see how the light on my mountain

allows our eyes to gather
the variegated COLORS?
I only thought to install windows
when I caught sight of that light

which will become His light not—
long from—now.   Storms
revealed the (secret) geologic
steps through which they had

to pass to become what they are.
That's why ze vindow . . .'
But would that same wise-
aleck learn—how—to

pronounce Goethe's name?
Maybe instead of having you memorize
who held what office and when
I should have striven to mesmerize

you with puzzling, ambiguous,
ultimately unsettled incidents
like what went on
between Wolfe and Montcalm.

*(They could stay up all night
memorizing and write down
answers and check off
boxes, but no one,*

*over a good—week—
giventuGermanhistry
could say his name right.
I think I even wrote it on the board*

*like this: Gurrrr—tuh . . .
They'd gotten the first syllable
because of the actor
who played goldsomething*

and that was enough.
What would you expect —
when the hawk running
for highest office,

was the Goldwater
whose department store
was their—second—home?
And whose two golden-haired

daughters they espied (in daylight
only) on these very premises.
Who knew from Goethe
in Goldwater land?)

What has all this got to do
with us? Only this:
that too was a time of violent change.
I think the sage says somewhere . . .

brrring . . .

Don't leave your seats just yet
ladies and gentlemen.
I know you think Goethe's a stuffed shirt,
but what if I told you that when he was four

he emptied all his mother's crockery
onto the street; the neighbor's applause
only made him throw more.
I know you're all daredevils now,

but can anyone in this room honestly say
they did something so outrageous, risking
what unknown recriminations? You can't copy
this answer from your classmates so stop

looking so frantically around the room.
Miss (he stares at seating chart) . . . Wilderness . . .
what would your mom have done
if you had tossed out her china?

(Racking cough) . . . Or some heirloom?
Taken away your TV privileges
for the afternoon?" (He chortles; class joins in.)
"Probably, sir, if she hadn't been a potter."

This brought down the house.
The class went out of control.
All except for Tory. And one other.
When the noise died down, Tory asked,

"What would your mother have done sir?"
"I'll share that with you gladly.
Broken my piggy bank,
hiked down to Woolworths."

5

Brrring . . .

The class runs out. He stands with his hands pressed to the back of his
chair, murmuring, "Goethe, Goethe . . ."

"The soul rises like water,
then comes back down
to earth like rain; never
the same, never

losing track of heaven.
Change is our guide.
Surprise—our habitat,
hour after hour.

Forever; now.
The battered cliffs
break the joint efforts
of earth air and sea-spray.

The soul of man
pours out like water.
And man's fate
is in the wind."

PHAETON'S DREAM:
DRIVING LESSONS IN THE DESERT

I

(Scene: A boarding school in the Sonoran desert. A teenage boy falls asleep reading Ovid in the library.)

Phaeton's big mouth got him into this.

If only
>he could have kept quiet about his royal lineage;

if only
>"deep-rooted" insecurity did not drip from him like sweat;

if only
>he had not provoked the Taunt of Epaphus

(Jove's son, and no slouch when it came to family trees).

But can changing the focus now affect what happened then?

It depends on what you mean by *then.*

As when time was time before we intersected.
Crossed over into. And became part of—not apart from.

You are led by faith. I will not stand in your way.

Phaeton's mother is a sunflower, alone among succulents.
Softly her voice penetrates the desert silence.

"I've spent my life trying to get Apollo on the line.
Sad waste. If you want an illustrious father, kid,

don't imagine he'll have time for children's games.
This is a man who calls only from the carphone.

But let no man say you are not the son of the sun.
Go seek His Radiance: I feel his rising's near."

The very words Phaeton wanted to hear.
"I never knew you were a mindreader.

I'd never thought the sun might *not* be my father.
Now this dark questionmark fills my head.

I'm not myself now, and won't be
until I know for sure one way or the other."

(Scene: PHAETON VISITS HIS FATHER'S DIGS)

It was time to find out what was what.
Who was who. Who he was. Or was not.

He lit out on his glittering Schwinn
for the headquarters of Mission Apollo—

a rotating dome fixed at the precise altitude
from where the eye could scan four states

and in an instant's telescopic flick-of-the-switch
close-in-on and blow-up any image. Bring the far off near.

Security was tight. Phaeton charmed the guards.
Heck, what harm could a boy on a bicycle do?

It wasn't sheer rashness that propelled Phaeton to show
up unannounced at his "father's" glass tower;

nor had he come for the commanding panoramic view of
Arizona, Colorado, Utah, and New Mexico.

*(But what other physicist both searched for life forms light
years away and fiddled with fusion to refine the . . . blasts . . . ?)*

(Scene: AT MISSION APOLLO)

Stacked clouds. Horizonless distances.
And yet no end to the radiance in his father's office:

Phaeton could not bear to see him face to face.
In his high chair above his solar-powered levers,

this *god* surveyed the desert. Skin greenly glittering.
("The flashings coming off him blinded me.

On the day I have an audience with my radiant father
I have to forget my mirror Ray Ban's, right?")

The northern lights stay far enough away.
Why couldn't the sun god be a little less like a Rotarian?

(Because my father's generation still values what others could bestow——.)"
Apollo welcomed his son, and waved his cell phone.

"I know you're anxious to take the wheel but can't we get to know
each other first? Do you like Dunkin' Donuts coffee?

I just ordered some. It's the best in town."
What's the right counter-banter? Why is he talking down?

"Yes. I always go there after the dentist."
"I'm thrilled to know that," Apollo comes back, flat-voiced.

Phaeton goes cold, then reasons with the full force of dream:
"Maybe my dad's voice didn't just go dead

when I said something about me, it could be his office-acoustics
which won't matter once I get ahold of the keys——."

"Son. Don't go. Get a hold. . . . There are other ways to verify . . . !
Would I have named The Phaeton The Phaeton if you were not
 Apollo's son?"

2

During the Roman-American merger the antique and the new
flowed through the lot packed with intergalactic

Galaxies, Furys, and Mercurys.
And then The Phaeton. Was it a car at all?

Or an idea whose body was forged out of car-parts?
The best and brightest parts from other autos

commingled on a chassis fashioned
from a captured asteroid: a mineral shield that will not burn.

Rack and pinion, bore and shake, hydraulic shocks.
An awed Phaeton gaped at the machine.

The globed instrument panel.
The retractable wings and pontoons.

And under the hood, layered and ornate, the chrome-plated
eight cylinder herd. The wild mustangs.

"They whinny when you turn it over."
(Horses who knew it was better to live without a body, than live

hounded by mercenaries, the merciless staccato bursts
of heat-sensitive machine guns,

the locust shadows cast by demonic
helicopters orbiting the open range.)

Why isn't Phaeton laying on the *oohs* and *aahs*?
His silence like an assassin.

Apollo breaks it: "It's a microcosm of what machines can do.
And since we can know everything that is going on everywhere

within this finite   space   only   time
stands between this partial knowledge of the world

and the whole

       CAKE

          to which I aspire.   "

         (Scene: APOLLO'S OFFICE)

"Forget ordinary gears. The Phaeton is designed
to adapt to changing conditions:

at these dizzying speeds your destination—
the very 'road' you're on—is a moving counter.

What's the mystery of the first hill if not that it gets steeper
as you go higher, car and hill parallel at the top,

and since you have to *flip* the car to make it over
the descent begins with free-fall and gets worse from there:

going down you're on fire; I have to say aloud
You're not burning up to make myself believe it."

"I'm not sure I understand."
"Think angles. Think rebound. Do you play pool?"

"I can clear the table. I'm the best at my school."
"Think—a physics of bank shots. The natural

curves of space run congruent to your ideal speed."
(Why is Apollo always clearing his throat,

sucking Tic Tacs and muttering that he's very dry?)
"What you're moving toward is moving toward you.

Keep your shoulder to the wheel, ignore the horses' tug
toward chaos and destruction and you'll be just fine. . . ."

"It'll be all right Dad, just give me the keys."
"How do I know you won't— . . . ."

"It's my birthright."

"You're not ready yet. This is not the car,
this is not the road, for you to practice driving on.

Know now I am your father by my fear.
I don't want my son to disappear.

Make a second wish. I'll grant it right away.
This *instant.* And we'll see what we can do

about your rash request when the time is—propitious—.
The road is thick with Terrors Strenuous.

The track is treacherous, rife with monsters
which swell in size as you gather speed:

the horns of the bull, the arrow of the archer,
the lion-with-fangs-bared; scorpion and crab

ferris-wheeling . . . ." Phaeton's *yes*
offered the sun-god cold comfort.

(Gods! They could sure go on.
The sun should put these step by step

instructions on tape; so I can take in
what is relevant when I reach that stage of my journey.

Advice is useless. Experience is all.)
"There won't be time to listen and react."

(Do gods read thoughts? Or are they . . . paranoid?)
"Don't hug me now to get what you want

when it's the last thing you should have.
I know how to settle this. Come, let's stand together

in the mirror." Spoken as if there weren't mirrors
positioned everywhere in Apollo's workspace

to guarantee he should never be alone.
"Resemblances aren't proof. I have to know

whether or not you ARE my father."
"One wish. Whatever you want."

"That's easy. To take The Phaeton out for a spin."
"Anything but . . . !"

"But you gave your word. Whatever I want."
"I'll try another route into your shaggy cranium.

Never mind the wildness of the horses,
the intricacy of the gadgets.

The bottom line is—you don't have a license.
We'll talk about it again when you turn sixteen."

"The driving age is 15½ where I come from."
"Why not let me take you up. That way

you can relax and observe the rites, the festivals,
the ultimate light-show in silence."

"No deal. Let me have the keys. Dad."

3

Horses are not stupid; just single-minded.
They know where they want to be.

Around the testing site it's wind thrumming in the wires.
"Dust in the wind," echoes the boy.

Was Phaeton listening? Why was he biting his lip?
Perhaps, like many teens, he was adept

at Doing Many Things At Once. Reciting his silent mantras
and fiddling with the gear-shift during

Apollo's cautionary sermon may not have kept
His Ears From Hearing.

My father sure likes the sound of his own voice.
I wonder who he talks to when no one's here to listen.

The sun-god rubbed Sunscreen 45 over his son's face.
"Don't press down hard on the accelerator.

Grip the wheel—hard—instead.
Stay away from the reactor's radar-grip."

4

"The wind outside was real and if I was to go
I was—to go now—before I had a sandstorm

to contend with beyond . . . what my father warned.
Sinking into The Phaeton's shaped seat

I couldn't have dreamed it better: a radio with no
earthly limit; but where to begin when you're free

to tune in on any station in the world?
If The Phaeton was mine I'd want to be in it

all the time; I'd *live* at Drive Ins."

5

Invisibility: a blessing to mischief.
The immortals get away with murder.

Phaeton remembered lines from the song
his classmates chanted in disorderly chorus

in protest to the canteen closing down:
"*We gotta get out of this place*

if it's the last thing we ever do. . . .
You don't believe we're on the eve of destruction."

The minor goddess assigned to the case pulled out the chocks
without a signal from the chief. The car

reared on its hind wheels as Phaeton peeled out
squealing, burning rubber.

Phaeton was that much lighter than Apollo!
Phaeton upside down—lucky to be strapped in!

Head under heels   a second takes a

LONG   TIME

your keys   and loose change   loosed
throughout the universe.

The horror fast began to dawn on Phaeton.
He could detect no order, no pattern.

Was the universe whirling the opposite way?
The car was still in first when the horses sensed

they had a lightweight—(a mere boy!)—at the wheel.
The mustangs bolted. The Phaeton careened.

Broad flat arroyos widen into monstrous maws.
Phaeton entered   NOWHERE.

Denver, Vegas, Albuquerque, Phoenix
blaze then darken. The wheel too hot to touch.

Phaeton breathed relief—too soon.
Before he—"saw stars."

♣

Earth white as paper.
Flat. Cartoonish.

The sky—silver—yellow—orange—

no, NO

Glow of ionized air. Light
whiplashing off new-formed clouds, in the lee

of shock waves, across the desert bowl
in silence; the distance,

expanding, cracks
like a pistol's sharp report.

The auras of the mustangs issue from the engine,
like electrons stepping out of atoms.

♣

With brands blazing, shape-shifting light,
the horses scatter like a pack of cards.

Revenge is messy: it spills onto the innocent,
as now, pilots nearing Vegas International,

trusting their eyes and not their radar screens,
mistook the rectangle of flames for a runway,

swooped down, converged, and burst into flames.
Revenge is messy. Sure, the horses wished

death on those who hunted them from the air,
but these Boeings lowering their landing gear

were chockfull of innocent civilians,
some of whom had even signed petitions

apropos the mistreatment of wild horses. . . .
Once the mechanism of revenge is sprung

it must bring down whatever's in its range.
Too late Phaeton grasped the malevolence of Apollo's mission.

"Make it look like an accident."
And grew up fast.

There are no accidents.
Only the world itself is accidental.

III

❧

DYING AND FLARING

JOAN AND JEAN

I

after Lepage's *Joan of Arc*

(In the year in which it was painted, 1879, Lorraine was lost to Germany. Lepage transposed the Joan who sided with the Dauphin against England, with a Joan the French needed now—now that Germany had taken Lorraine.)

This a Joan who would appear at home in the salon,
sturdy, not unworldly;

a Joan the painter might have known.

She rises from the spinning wheel
in the autumnal tones of
the windfall orchard
wearing a gray dress.
Bound at the waist.

Golden haze of saints in the scaffolding.

A girl he might have watched wandering the German-

French border alone, a tomboy
whom he might have leched after or
enjoyed for her bristling, robust spirit?

It's a leap to dress Joan in a dress—

given her insistence on wearing what men wore
when she led them into battle—

although she did request one

before entering the fire—

She was used to going barefoot
and so didn't have to think twice
about running to her death in bare feet.

*But I thought you were interested in Lepage because of your mother's side
of the family: The Alsace-Lorraine connection.*

Sounds like a potboiler.

A cliffhanger.

(Pause.)

I don't care. There's a golden blaze in it!

You come from a divided tribe.

2

We could call the other, for symmetry's sake, Jeanne Seberg,

*Jean was, after all, if not immolated, at least
burned, scarred, scalded, during the pyre
scene of* Saint Joan, *to the apparent pleasure
of the sadistic director. Herr Otto Preminger.*

Chorus:

Blame him, blame him.
Saint Joan was a disaster.
Jean Seberg became a star.

Jeanne D'Arc was a martyr.
Jean Seberg—a suicide.

Jean's activism doesn't count? It's too—secular?

Jean Seberg did not become a Christian martyr. But the short-
cropped hair remained her signature long after *Saint Joan* was a con-

firmed box-office flop. And she became the cunning teen in *Bonjour Tristesse*, the warrior's helmet converted to a red towel wrapped around her head.

The betrayer with the innocent face.

It was that quality that Godard identified. He knew he wanted to see what was behind Belmondo's tough-guy mask. And he wanted to show that the androgynous young woman running breathlessly up and down the Champs Élysées in a T-shirt and jeans hawking the *Herald Tribune*, was also not what she appeared to be.

But there is also the lovely scene when they're briefly alone together in a room, when she recites the last lines from The Wild Palms, *"Between grief and nothing I will take grief," in a kind of reverie.*

Her French was charming in its deliberateness—she put her lack of fluency to good use.

No two stories
or cases
are comparable?

Chorus:

Joan on the pyre.
Jean on the pyre.

Pain is weirdly relative.
Jean, the actress playing Joan,
felt flames lick her skin
while the camera was running,
and she counted on rescue
by the crew. . . .

So Jeanne and Joan
share something . . .

Jean loved Joan's France, the cathedral
at Rheims, Vaucoleur, and Rouen,
where Joan met her end and had her ashes
scattered in the river.

You were too young to have been privy
to the brouhaha about the fire singeing
her stomach, knees, and the backs of her hands
when the seven gas cylinders
hidden under the mound of faggots
that didn't go off at first . . .

Joan's priorities didn't revolve around Joan;
she, the original fearless girl, laid claim
solely to the voices she heard in the orchard,
and acted like the vehicle
for the urgent call to arms
it had fallen on her to relay.

They found unnerving
this impartial, if reluctant
witness to a human
situation she refused
to accept.

But to think she even got near the Dauphin, who was hardly in the
mood to hear her dark prognostications! Imagine a girl from Neb-
raska being granted an audience with the Joint Chiefs of Staff.

(But I'm sure that the Kennedys, and even McNamara and Rusk, would
have taken up *with Jean Seberg if she had asked to see them with regard*
to the Black Panthers, whose case she had taken up.

Probably.

Even if she hadn't had a cause they would have found a way to use her.)

3

My friend's friend is a sound engineer whose luck it was to record
Bob Dylan, in a working session, singing "Ring of Fire"
again

again and again, differently each time, chatting with the musicians
between takes, "let's give it a whack, give it a bash . . ."

His tape to tape had broken down so he lent me the original
and, while overcome with fatigue at this endless winter's end,
and I longed for dogwood, locust, magnolia, cherry tree and plum
to burst into flower, something in me gave way,
broke, I ceased
to resist;
I listened to that
                          chant of descent

"DOWN DOWN DOWN
And the FLAMES they went HIGHER"

and then she appeared, and drew near,
in this cold, dark, empty room in winter.

After she goes up in flames she looks down.
Earth flares. Everywhere a horrific blue abyss.

The straw catching fire, dry, at the end of summer.
The straw, wet, not catching fire, and the martyr forced to endure

the righteous jostling each other for the best view
as the flames, mounting higher, peel the clothes

from her firm young body;

the girl waiting for the gods

who are

nowhere,

having abandoned the sky forever.

Chorus:

Why is the sky now empty of gods
as it was for Andromache
when we would have them intervene
and put an end to an innocent's
burning, burning.

"That ring of fyre, that ring of fyre."

The end is the same even for those who escaped immolation, the Shaws, the Dreyers, the De Sicas, the Premingers, the countless act-resses and extras who've attempted to record her passage toward death.

Would it matter, when she was already dead?

Come again?

When she had already pronounced herself dead?

Huh?

When in her own mind she was to ALL INTENTS AND PURPOSES dead.

She was no stranger to waiting. It took her over five hundred years to become a saint.

Which the poet of the Vaucluse, René Char, found suspect.

Joan Burned Green

The canonization of Joan of Arc?
No theologian or man of god, my thoughts move elsewhere.

But I would have fought alongside that young girl, near her, for her,
because, in her time, she was right to conjoin mysticism and rebellion.

Sometimes I think of what her physical presence was like.
(It is nothing like the testimony of the witnesses at her trial.)

Torso cut into a vertical rectangle, like a plank of walnut.
Arms long and vigorous. The Latin hands still evolving.

No ass at all. As if her buttocks refused to fill out
when she sensed she would wage war.

Her face the opposite of barren.
An extraordinary presence, emotional authority.

A living mystery. No breasts at all. Vanquished
by her chest. Two hard ends. Flat high stomach.

Back smooth and supple, like an apple tree's trunk;
energy over muscle, yet hard—like a ram's horn. Her feet!

After wandering long in the hoofprints of a fattened herd,
we see them rise with shocking force

to attack the flanks of war horses, beat back
the invaders, trace the nomad choice of a place

to pitch camp . . . , and in the end her reward was to endure
the afflictions suffered by the soul tortured and driven into solitary.

This is translated in terms of *earth*, the "green earth of Lorraine,
battle-weary, blood on the ground,"

there remains "the sacred earth of Reims.
Pale, hospitable to—dungeons. Earth of

the untouchables. Earth glimpsed below
the pyre's wood. Earth blazed.

Earth maybe utterly blue in her aghast
glance. —Ashes—."

4

Tears pour from Anna Karina's face during the pyre scene in *Vivre sa Vie* when she retreats to the cinema to view Carl Dreyer's *Joan of Arc*. It's relentless: Falconetti's shaved head, her bloodshot eyes, white walls, black robes. And the young, unravaged Antonin Artaud, whispering to her of paradises elsewhere, adds another dimension of tragedy beyond the film itself that Dreyer couldn't have predicted.

Why would the scrupulous Robert Bresson have made another film about Joan after the matchless Dreyer . . . ?

Sound. And that when in prison the most important thing is the door.

There'd be counterpoint:
the sound of cell
doors clanging and the cutting back and forth

between French and English
voices,

(he used the actual
transcripts)

dogbark, chain-
clank, discrete

elements, her feet
in isolation, her expression
when the three women
lift the covering sheet to
check out her virginity
again,

monks' robes, soldiers' uniforms,

the English straining to glimpse

through cracks in cell walls
the girl, when—

God help them—

she isn't looking;

the fatal drumroll.

There's no escape
from what the seer sees.

And there's no way

around recurrence;

the seer must pay.

5

There were times when people saw her everywhere;
places she'd never set foot in.

There may have been sightings.

I do not know, and yet the sci-fi "sightings,"
imbue them with questionable, if not specious

powers, and fueled the arguments against
her being pardoned:
it is her "image" that makes her so dangerous.

Present tense dangerous?
Just so.

The Bishop had no right to call for private interrogation; some of the
prelates walked out of the trial in protest.

Her story's unfinished.
And not because she died at seventeen,
or her heart scorned fire— . . . it's that her ultimate
intentions, the method behind
the discourse
                    were never taken for more
than cunning, artful delusion.

Innocence her passport to ruin.

It comes down to faith. Either you believe
she opens a door onto a mysterious world and then
closes it, or you don't; and if you don't
then you're in league with the forces of right.

(And the still unborn—Age of Reason.

Which we're still trying to unravel.
Like Rousseau's shock
when he happened on
a stocking-mill factory
in "virgin forest"?)

But to think that at the end she was still concerned for the souls of her
prosecutors.

What God might not do to them!

Rider's Postscript to "Joan"

Of course you've read Michelet on Joan.

Not.

I see. It's fine for Mark to make things up, to see things as he pleases, but not for a great historian like Michelet whose history, I mean histories, of France are increasingly vilified for inaccuracy.

And he is only another indelible source I pressed upon you to consult before you lost yourself

in casuistry, the indeterminate adrift,
in smokeless fire, in fashion, in malign uncertain
      pluralisms, which

—amount—

    to subtracting intuition whenever
      doubt is sighted and nailed down
    like a computer virus.

Foray is the operative word.

That's good, as long as you stay clear of . . .
    military connotations. . . .
Forays in the South Pacific Theater meant
    certain . . . death . . .

to the unwary!

The keenest quester has to sleep sometime. The will is never more than . . .

World and Idea, as if life's orchestra offered more!

Michelet was neither wrong nor right. But if you'd read his book on Joan you wouldn't have had to ask if Jeanne D'Arc was attractive. Canny, intuitive, Jules Michelet (unlike your infinitely less significant Jules Bastien-Lepage, your painter for people who care more for the what than the how) isn't remembered for his gaffes, which no one beyond fellow explorers-in-the-field can identify anyway.

Or magic. Don't forget *La Sorciere.* That one I do know.

Or that, with regard to Joan, he treats her as not all that far out for the time.

Magic's contagious?

Or are there times in human history
when the ineffable baits its hook,
when the miraculous stands at ease
alongside the commonplace?

No one, neither Moses, Blake nor the saints to come
can ever count on being visited.

And don't forget Elijah's cup.
His thirst is not defined by limits;

a fool is one who measures the amount of wine
missing from His cup, the silver

chalice you let that diehard eternal outsider/wanderer
drink from and drain every time Passover traces its own

reoccurrence, and the story, once
again, compels both the avid listeners

and those who have no time for time,
that sector which, more fatigue-stricken than malicious,

masking desperation with such a masterful
imitation of being there in more than body,

only long, beyond language
to recline, as the service will, in time,

enjoin them. The prayers bless relaxation.
Slouching; slithering.

So you never held it against me that during one of those early Passovers over which you presided—perhaps the first one at which I was required to play my assumed role as your somewhat interested (in the proceedings), diligent and responsible "son," the thick, scratchy, woolen pants Mom demanded I wear to look correct began to burn and itch so much I could no longer cope, so I crawled under the table and pulled your socks down and tickled your ankles and whispered "let's go!" and when you didn't so much as tap a response, I tied your shoelaces together, crawled out and onto the stage and fell dead asleep behind the drawn curtain.

Not if you don't hold it against me that I didn't really notice until it was time to leave and your mother, in that wry way she once had, said quietly, and without a trace of worry, "I wonder where the child is. Where do you think it is?"

When you stood up, I heard the crash.

There was no crash.

You buckled forward onto the card table. It collapsed. I heard the crash.

No, I simply knelt down, untied the knots, which I wasn't until now aware that YOU had tied (though in retrospect who else could it have been), and regained my equanimity.

You weren't angry?

No, people were scurrying everywhere, clearly happy with how the service had gone and even a little high from all those slugs of sweet wine and talk of freedom; besides, Passover isn't a night on which I would see fit to punish acts of mischief. You seem to forget that I knew my Freud—I expected certain acts of hostility from you towards me—and I didn't expect you to behave like a model anything.

Rider's Postscript to "Jean"

I know how fragile your relationship to reality is.

Not so.

Oh I don't mean it in a clinical sense. It's your inclination to leave out . . .

But what makes you bring it up now?

How odd it is, given the role you've already allotted Brecht in this work, that you should neglect to list him along with those who've portrayed the woman-warrior from Lorraine. Saint Joan of the Stockyards *may not be in the same class as Shaw's play, but—*

Sometimes rhythmical thinking takes over and incantation overwhelms information.

And you don't follow through on the parallels between the martyred saint's fate and that of the future Jean "Saber," warrior for the radical left . . .

who in taking on the Black
Panthers as her personal cause,
inherited the nemesis
who, obsessed with celebrities,
took a special interest in her case,
who made her life hell
and hounded her to death,
using means to cause maximum
humiliation and fear
so he, J. Edgar Hoover
could savor the unraveling;
her pain.

(Pause.)

My will waned. I don't like these prescriptive do's and don'ts. You're not suggesting I should have shifted the focus . . . you're still peeved that I never read that novel by Seberg's husband, Romain Gary.

You mean Genghis Cohen? *Why should I care if you read it or not? Or know about dybbuks or anything else in the vanishing of Yiddish culture? And did I ever say anything when I saw you wasting your time on . . .*

Stop fencing with me!

Ah, so I did touch a nerve. Remember what
your "Pop-Pop" said: "da noives."

(Pause.)

No one could say you were ever
anything less than nervous.

I think you mean restless.

Don't interrupt!
Let's skip any intermediate distractions:
you can't encompass Jean Seberg
without so much as mentioning
her far-more-worthwhile-as-a-subject husband.

So far, the quarrel's all on your side.

What quarrel? I'm just anticipating
objections north of the future.
But you're . . . resistant as ever.

The Ski Bum spoiled me for further Gary.

Did The Misfits *spoil you for further Miller?*

Let's just say that a lot of the story took place outdoors in a landscape I
loved.

What story?

"The Misfits."

Never heard of it. But I saw the original Death of a Salesman, *with Lee J.*
Cobb now that was . . .

(Pause.)

Did Mark take advantage of Utah's
slopes? No, but Mark watched countless skiers schuss

off, vanish, and return to the heights
over and over again, yet he still imagined
that the very slopes Easterners would kill
to go down are concave, bent on hurtling
his hyper-sensitive frame into empty space
and death upon sudden impact . . . the same
"little boy Mark" who felt no compunction
when it came to dirt-biking in the desert
and going over high cliffs
which weren't intended for sport . . .

I'll try to ignore the tone but need time to compose a response.
It's time that you began to see the larger context.

You're the boss.

(Pause.)

I had driven you to the airport the day
Marilyn's death made the headlines.

The front page of every major newspaper in the world
strewn like flyers . . .

between Marilyn's dark night and your late
morning flight.

I was disturbed. She was too young to die.

She didn't, any more than Mademoiselle "S" . . .

I don't mean age. I mean readiness for death.

She was meshuga. *Terrified of aging.*
Now you know what "fucked out" really means.

Yeah, that it doesn't mean.

Except that everyone has to pay.
No act goes unrecorded.

(Pause.)

What do people want from other people?

I think it was Ingrid Bergman—now there was a real actress—
who remarked that each new Joan has her hair cropped
closer to her skull.

What do people want from other people?

That Dior saleswoman
who suggested a wig to go with
a black satin dress Jean had chosen
to wear at some gala where she would meet,
among others, Françoise Sagan.

Insensitivity knows no boundaries.

No national boundaries.

Didn't you once drag me to a movie
in which Seberg played a psychoanalyst's
wife? And wasn't that suave headshrinking
paragon infected with the affectless self-conceit

endemic and epidemic to a profession
which encourages those "certified (or certifiable) doctors"
to play god when they should pray to god?

You're straying.

But the weasel did blithely and blindly
place his career
over any concern for her?

Maybe.

He kept her waiting all the time as your father did you.
If you'd read your Heidegger you'd know that carelessness
is not to be taken lightly.

No no no. You grouped Heidegger
with existentialists who "couldn't hold a candle"
to your men who placed essence over existence;
but on one of my early trips to Greenville,
I got you to read one of his late essays
and, walking the muddy delta after rain,
we discussed how he used
the caked dirt on Van Gogh's shoes.

I did think the existential vision was a step backward,
since essence assumes existence,
but I wasn't dismissive and often assigned
Sartre's The Anti-Semite and the Jew *to my reading groups . . .*

Wait! Dirt on shoes: human use.
Seberg's essence was her absence.
Something impalpable.
No stray hairs on the pillow.

I know you know the film I mean because your hero,
that burrish Scotsman—are they all named Sean?—trying . . .

(I knew a girl who pronounced his name Seen.

How did she do with Sinead? Was that . . . that Laura?)

everything to escape being typecast forever as "Bond,
James Bond," (always a cipher to me except
for his fetishes) played a mad wild poet
run amuck in Manhattan.

(Pause.)

There are other curious factors in Seberg's case. Seberg could have written a lot of her own lines in *A Fine Madness*. Such as these rejoinders to her husband and her lover.

"I'll meet you in an hour."
"One hour your time is about six hours standard time."

"What do you know about Apollo?"
"Some of us intake valves have read a little."

"Swords are men's weapons," Seberg says in the *Journals*, "women have vaginas."

That poet was a bully and a lout . . .

Samson Sillitoe was probably modeled on the half-bards
who were as well known for disregarding
certain tacit social codes—like don't fuck
your host's wife in the pauses between courses—

but he couldn't have predicted that Jean's
only too debonair, controlled, careering
"husband," a classic "later dear later"
kind of—man?—would look in when she and Sean
stripped, stepped into the whirlpool, and frolicked,
with no reason to think they might be seen.

I remember a window like that
attached to my dad's room
during his sojourn in the bin.

You're still obsessed with his demise.

No. Only with its suddenness.

*But neither he nor Jean wanted
to be released back into life's
chaotic stream.*

Don't you mean scream?

You were never so avid for answers as now.
Is there nothing you'll consent to leave unsaid
out of some respect for the dead?

The mystery of suicides
demands some consolation
given life's intractable givens.

Anyone can choose death over
life, but this grove of suicides
had something to live for.

Why can't you accept that Jean
had exhausted her life's options . . . ,
aided by the toxic mixture of early success
and midwestern Lutheranism.

The chess game had come to an end.

And her wager, like Pascal's
(who was addicted to gambling)
was rooted in the physical;
and while her bets were not quite real
she staked her life on their success;
"reality" to actors
means assuming roles, disguises;
being means being another.

What's luck without felicity?

It's as if some demon dragged her down
for being the one girl chosen
out of three thousand to play Joan.
And for becoming an icon in the first New Wave film.

So, at each decisive turn in her life,
Jean landed in the hands of three
shameless European misogynists.
Preminger, Godard, Gary.

Three years after he shattered illusion in *Breathless*
by having Jean look directly at the viewer,
Godard cast her as a documentary filmmaker
in a short film called *Le Grand Escroc:*
here she's the observer, not the observed,
like Joan interrogating her inquisitors.

In this film about swindling,
cinema itself is shown to be the greatest lie.

In the blinding light of Marrakech slums
she fixes her camera on a living
paradox: a counterfeiter
who distributes phony bills to the poor
and calls it charity.

Her husband, like many other estimable men,
was demented when it came to women.

More than Roger Vadim
who Barbie-dolled Jane Fonda?

Vadim practically created the "sex-kitten" with Bardot.
It's different when a serious
writer takes his first turn behind the camera
by casting his wife as a nymphomaniac

so he can . . . watch.

Objection. The prosecution will concede that he is offering an opinion . . . ?

Yes, your honor, if it will mollify
the defense.

Seberg had always refused to appear nude.
But her face in the sex scenes
in Gary's Eurotrash potboiler, *Birds of Peru*,
became an agonized mask.
And how would the audience know
that the body-double was not she?

So now her bleak fate is all Gary's fault?
You make her sound like a luckless wretch.
Hecuba without years.
If Jean had absorbed some of her future
husband's famous books or their film versions,
she might have known better
than to marry a man to whom
all women were whores.

In *Roots of Heaven* Gary's alter-ego explains
he'd waited all his life for someone
to spit on him, and the character exclaims:
"Now it's almost bearable to be a man."

I think it was Gary who left her after she . . . became too friendly . . .
with Clint Eastwood while filming *Paint Your Wagon*.

That's where one of her lines is: why can't a woman be married to two
men.

It bothered the Mexican novelist whom she met around that time
that she placed a headshot of Clint, with an unlit cigar between his
tightly shut lips, on his nightstand.

It wouldn't bother you I suppose?

The novelist lived with her on location
while she was shooting a western
near Santiago, a backwater
where boot-camp haircuts were the fashion
and resembled the local ravines.

The novelist was no Candide or Clouseau
but prior to this affair had been innocent of
fruit-flavored vaginal creams,
peach, strawberry, pineapple, orange,
that brought back childhood memories

of mango and guava ice-cream dissolving
on his tongue . . . and long after
her body was found
decomposed in the backseat of her white Renault
on the ill-lit, obscure Rue du General Appert

he still treasures the marmalade jar
where her pubic hair is preserved
along with the scent of her lubricants.

STEALTH

Venice in winter: a history of disappearances. Loved faces lost.

Othello was here more briefly than I remember, it's all
mixed up,
            the moor's
                        (so-called) permanent residence
and where he woos Desdemona,
and the Cyprus interval.

These fictions of yours are mere gambits.

That's all I'm ever after. As they used to say to double-agents setting
out on impossible missions, "stealth and secrecy are our only hope."

Have you ever heard of the Completion Complex?

I've heard the phrase, but it takes more than a rhyming prefix to make
a complex.

Not universal enough? There aren't
enough people in the world whose problem
is they can't seem to complete what they've begun,
from intercourse to—the projects
that define their lives . . . ? Surely you can fill in
examples from your own . . . experience . . .
in the global sense. . . .

Would you agree that finishing something
is a kind of dying, a moment whose
sigh, even of satisfaction, brings on
spectral thoughts, anxiety, "what next?"

There's value in this emptiness.

Yes, but in the disoriented instant,
as when you lose your way in a winter
fog in Venice
              when you're on an errand,

in time for . . . it doesn't matter what . . .
and what might otherwise be pleasingly
unfamiliar, becomes like a bad dream
from which you can't will yourself to awaken

and you can't write it off as a failure:
your clenched fist grips the paper bag
which contains the simple remedy for
the traveler-friendly malaise which
condemned your lover, (wife or child), to waiting,
waiting in one of its purest
forms, what with the room
reeling, the child channel-surfing
to the rhythm of waves breaking against the Zattere
quay, the woman thwarted in her attempts to focus
to get her eyes to focus
on the page, whose sequential
words, wheeling like the gulls whose cries you can hear
even now, appear to mock—

if not this woman, alone in the room—
the absurdity of having tried
to somehow prepare for situations
whose chaos is the essence. . . . Of Venice.

Of the man who laid his hands on
the equilibrium restoring medicine
by crossing just one more bridge,
and saw no reason why
(—It was all so easy!—)
he might return by
a bridge just like the one
she crossed without a
hitch—when it appeared to run
parallel—it wasn't as if she were dying

or something, to set foot in the room when she
was so out of it meant
missing the possible
mystery in the unfolding,

in the fogged-in city
in this created maze.

Your concern with getting lost
borders on the fatuous.

Considering you are a world away from Venice.

Physically, now.

Poised beside the Battenkill
wondering whether to watch or jump in.

2

It is the end of summer—

So what's stopping—

Wind high in the sycamores,
pheasants surging ahead en route

to nowhere   the road
bends, and rises, and falls
with seductive allure;

another instance of life
no, landscape
imitating art, as each bend
replicates and recalls
Cézanne's *Bend in the Road.*

But there the weather never changes.
It's always early fall and the leaves
having changed color are still
remote from the picturesque.

It was a "brace of pheasants,"
flock being too common, herd disproportionate,
pride inappropriate, bunch slovenly . . .
gaggle too goose specific.

I wonder why brace seemed right when it applied to only
two, not five or six . . .

Your nature skills are rusty;
and you half-suspected they were
quail and avoided that blunder
by reimagining the pheasant
trapped inside the tennis court at dusk
in Paterson, New York in late
October

and the others you knew
from walks in the surrounding woods.

And now one rises, big-bellied,
beating wings
                    too small to do more

than move low and slow over
the meadow while its companions
move together, in a pack,
across the open field in the sun.

More stealth is warranted.

Gunshots.

In August?

Crack.

Quail drop from the sky.

The pheasants didn't appear cautious,
but they moved with greater stealth
than the quail who thrashed in the brush
like a demented percussion section.

I thought there had to be many many
more than there were.

I've heard the coyotes howling in the night.
Maybe a pack of coyotes would hesitate
before attacking a quail battalion.

There was something dignified about their stride,

strategic quail command,
attacking together in one downward
strike, savaging fur with beaks.

There'll be moments when only nature
will recognize the snow-covered, muddy,
brown-leaf strewn mound as that once luminous
site . . .

What nature?

Depends if you're talking northern Vermont or North Dakota.

Monadnock or the Black Hills.

Or the lightning storm from which you never recovered.

The storm I couldn't recapture.

Or capture on film. With your still camera.

The storm I couldn't catch up with.

Driving all out through the Black Hills.

Rhode-Island sized cloud-mat, lightning laddering down,
the empty spaces fully empty, utterly at ease, not one
animal or human dwelling in sight.

The distances we covered at more
than a mile a minute were scorned by the storm
that remained fifty miles ahead and moving away.

And I saw reinforcements arriving on horseback,
whose hearts rise upon sighting the battle site
when they realize they can't reach it in time
to do more than bury the dead.

It's like an optical illusion but it isn't.
Like distances at sea.

THE LAST NIGHT OF A FIRST TRIP TO VENICE

Awakened in the dead of night by the clatter
Of cloudy panes, I hurried to the window.
Rows of gondolas rocking on the swells.
Absence pressed heavily against the oars.

An arpeggio struck from a guitar
Made me search the sky, where a three-pronged spear
Blazed above the horizon, watery,
Gray, and where the sun scattered no ashes.

The zodiac strikes the lonliest chords.
Undaunted, the harbor went on with this
Misty shape-shifting as if the trident
Didn't exist. And no one else to witness!

Land and sea split off. Palaces capsized.
A planetary fortress was sighted.
Houses whirled, but while it looked like chaos,
They returned, like the planets, to their sites.

As the day began to break I began
To grasp that Venice was also adrift
In the midst, in the blurred boundary
Between so-called reality and dream.

Growing more surefooted with every step,
I crossed bridges I couldn't see. I heard
The far off whispers of conspirators.
I saw myself on Marburg's cobblestones—

The day I blurted out to Hermann Cohen
That I was giving up philosophy,
And would soon depart for Venice.
I braced myself. "Logic is not for everyone

Maybe you'll find your way around the haze
That separates us from the things themselves."
"In Venice there is metamorphosis.
Boundaries are erased. Stone becomes porous."

And like a blossom in the throws of foam,
And like a rabid foaming at the lips,
A chord sounded in the shadowy vague.
The who and where and why didn't matter.

(after Boris Pasternak)

WITHOUT A CARE IN THE WORLD

Venice doesn't have a history; it is history. Who can keep track of the armies that have come and gone.

If only Freud had lit upon Venice instead of Rome as a model of the mind we might all be saved.

An increase of syllables will not increase
the number of stars, or dust particles, or pollen.

Even I, who never liked Fellini's films
         after he became a traitor to black and white
adored *Casanova*—or was it Venice?—
         when Casanova sails
across canals of garbage bags.

You've neglected every opening to bring in Turner.

I've nothing against him, and am not unmoved by the story of how as a young man he was strapped to the mast in a terrible storm.

Then why this silence.

Constable—snatched my body.

The deference pain insists on.

No matter what—extremity is listed.

You make it sound like a religious conversion.

With Constable there's still the tension of the things themselves, the gnarled and knotty cottages and trees, the leaf swirl as the fisherman, man or boy, wades into the stream, casting, his line lost amidst the cloud flecks; the gentry stiff in civilized discourse beside the immaculate cathedral, and those who work the land, maintain the grounds,

laughing muddily on riverbanks where no one looking the other way
can see them. Constable tried to paint what he saw—but he was luck-
ily overwhelmed

by the pressure to express everything
    that was happening at once,
how the landscape changed
    in the twinkling of an eye,
and the challenge was then to render
    interruptions, like a child
who at one moment sleeps beside you,
    compact, wrapped
in a quilt, and the next moment
    stretches, spreads
his limbs, and takes over every inch of
    sleeping surface.

The fields remain, the locks and mills no longer used.

Without a Care in the World: (after Constable's Hay-on-Wye)

It is an end to walking on the fens
on gray afternoons at first flowering,
when a boy and his dog could stride
the knee-high heather alone together
harvesting the day because its dangers
lay elsewhere, like the distances under
new ownership, where a spire

is granted no more height or clout
than a windmill's one white, erect blade.
Elsewhere the edge, shorn of
cliff's cleavage, where land breaks off and sea
takes over, a line so clear as to shear
the sheer—the drop from land's end to beachhead
where all is whirling intervals—skyey

clouds, skeletal logs,
riverstream inland waterway
angler's line lost in stalks
(though he holds his rod like a bow),
as light rives the cottage roof and the gnarled
oak in the yard, the world given back
to the world.

MIDSUMMER NIGHT IN VENICE

What's the use of a Midsummer Night's Dream
without trampolines?

A diffuse, undirected aroma wafts through Venice tonight.

Perhaps the gods have not abandoned
these cathedral vaults.
The bells ring on time.
Eternal time.
Now.

Dreams surpassing explanations.

All—bottomless—

for the same reasons.

"There is no falling here . . ."

I have this sense that I am surrounded
by people falling in love with each other again,
familiars finding new qualities to marvel at—
as if they hadn't allowed their gaze to light on
their chosen mates for centuries.

Not years?

No, millennia.

Shadows in the dream green light.
Canal-ripple.

Who did the lightning?

My legs and feet can't keep pace with my desires.

Don't be ashamed. The water's there to foster illusions.

TELL ME WHY

I see no reason why the site of this excursus
just had to be Venice.

There are so many other places you might have chosen.
If you had kept an open mind and
used your noggin.

But you always had a hard head.
In more ways than one.

Oh hell, I was in Venice, I stayed at the Gritti—
I bet they wouldn't let you into the bar.

Then you did well on your Rabbi's salary.

It was a tour. I saw more in three days than you'd see in three weeks.

Venice is a tourist trap, and hideously expensive.
You could do so well for half the money in_____
*   or_____*

I like the mists and fog.

Look out the window will you man, Manhattan has enough fog and mist
for two of you. Haven't you often noted, losing yourself in meditation on
the cross-town bus, that in weather like this, damp, warm, misty, that
(utterly accessible) Central Park is like a primeval world, dense, dark,
unfathomable? A place as appropriate to dinosaurs as to ourselves.

Yes.

Then why Venice where, as that poet with the girl's middle name has it,
by late autumn . . .

It doesn't drift like bait any more, this city,
reeling in the days as they surface and flash.
The harder you look the harder the glass
palaces shake. The spent summer hangs

from garden fronds, like puppets thrown
in a pile, crumpled, beyond fatigue. . . .

in lines scribbled down prior to Dachau if I still have my dates   in order

Long before, but I hadn't thought of those heaped puppets in just that
way before.

There's a lot you haven't thought about.
Even by May of 1912
there were too many tourists in Venice
to satisfy Rilke's passion for solitude.

Don't you remember that one reason you chose
to stay in the desert
                                as long as you could,
given the limited decision making power
you had in those tender years—
was to clear your lungs,
to send your asthma
into hibernation
to   breathe — ?

And in addition to your mad wild inexhaustible
love of open spaces,
                                you used each occasion
to drive further and further from the city
limits, you rebelled
       against boundaries.

You and your friend, the one they nicknamed The Phantom, *were never*
   home.
Except to chow down.

The Phantom supplied the Corvair and I supplied the gas.

And you'll remember your father was the one
with the east east east *mantra who*
opposed your finishing high school in the desert

while I—since I was the one who had to drag
you to the doctors when you wheezed—went along
with your wishes.

There was something alluring about the idea of all that nothing beyond the surrounding mountains.

And yet you longed to return.

All I have to do is say a word and you're back on the street again,
vagabond ragamuffin.

A day of cold rain is no obstacle; it is an enticement, even though I still get nervous when I detect a slight wheeze in my lungs. Last week's downpour of light—so dazzling I could hardly shield my eyes from the glare. Now I'm also grateful for this dark downpour, the thump of windshield wipers, the blur of traffic lights. I'm curious to see who's doing what, who resorts to umbrellas, who carries on, oblivious, lugging shopping bags on Broadway as the wet paper looks like it will soon detach from the handles and remain on the street while the carrier continues home, not empty-handed, but with nothing more to show than handles.

The world rhythmically dying and flaring up again. You're looking ahead
to New Year's Eve when fireworks light up Rome's seven hills.

You're right. There are all the reasons in the world not to go to Venice. Maybe the fragility of its future provoked me into thinking differently about history. Here the devastation is so palpable. The drips and leaks. The rheumatic gutters.

It's a place where extremities reveal themselves: where the extreme emotions stand in the foreground.

The pendulum swings from gaiety to language. Where else but in Venice would you find a middle-aged couple, clearly on marriage number two, three, or . . . behaving this way, meandering hand and hand on the Zattere, dressed auspiciously in white, their light hair lit by flares.

What would happen if you kept your eyes open beginning say, tomorrow morning, when you stop for a corn muffin and a cafe con leche at the Rosita beside Straus Park on 107th St. instead of the Rosati on the Piazza del Popolo? Maybe it's a state of mind, not the place. . .

EARLY DELIVERIES NO ONE RECEIVES

("The United States and three other nuclear powers
negotiating a comprehensive ban on atomic testing
would all allow tiny blasts. But they disagree on the size
that should be permitted."
The New York Times, March 29, 1995)

for W. B.

Here's wishing the rain had gone on longer,
that the beat of windshield wipers
had continued to delight my renegade

eye, the goldenrod of taxis gone on
to flower against the uniform
dun March morning, the facades

time dressed in mourning.
Now it comes back, last night's dream:
you were disguised as that blind sage

whose detectives also had a way of
divining patterns in opaque terrain.
And since this rainy moment cannot recur

it's transparent that no one coming after us
will solve the puzzle of the UPS boxes
hurled pell-mell by men in brown

synthetic outfits onto wet, black asphalt,
one marked <INVOICE ENCLOSED>,
the other, <HANDLE WITH CARE>.

Here's wishing this pyramid were not attached
to the grimpen-tinted van—oblong monolith
emblazoned with obsequious gold lettering—:

like the bold young boy roller-blading Broadway alone
in the ratty dawn, scant trace of a cryptogram
"o   k   w t   me" ("don't fuck with me"?)

across the red (salmon-pink
from many washings?)
papyrus of his jersey.

Why pick this boy's silence
out of a crowd? Because he scorns
too much self-concern? Recognition

is everything. But the water
laving the wrought iron rail
of the Saxony Hotel as I cross

the cross street has a lovely,
lulling, momentarily calming . . .
something . . . I don't want to end.

And this downpour is blessedly outside
introspection's damaged arteries.
But so are the boxes, all shapes and all

sizes, no two alike!, piling up
around the—driverless—truck,
whose gilded grid, magisterial

from the Equator to the polar
cap, is topped by a topmost box
topped by a copy of today's

New York Times—if my eyes do not
betray my sight as I'm forced to squint—:
ATOMIC BLASTS, **or** Atomic Blasts?

IV

THE RETURN

VENICE: THE RETURN IN WINTER I

Destination: Venice: The Flight to Milan

This Christmas day the child and I are again
among a half-dozen on the packed
Boeing who keep watch through the long night.

Madelaine sleeps with Andrew Vachss's
Strega in hand, as if in mid-sentence.
And the quick-eyed, voluble

Italian woman with whom I waited
face to face in the vestibule
is now comatose under the blue blanket

she pulls over her eyes. Married to an
American, they live in Austin;
she misses Italy "in some ways, not all.

Nowhere else in Europe, perhaps on earth,
is there another people who still value
the quality of life over the glittering

temptations. I love American movies.
There's no glamour in Italian films and I'm
'up to here' with the poor . . . , always the poor."

Another woman is spread across an entire
middle aisle: her face as raw and harrowed
as one of Breughel's harvesters.

There's something suspect about people
who can fall asleep anywhere.
Three strong swigs of Jameson's and a knockout root-

canal-pain-killer a dear friend lent me
to quell the terrors of this night
flight over the devouring sea

bring me no closer to drowsiness;
besides, do you think the child and I would miss
the "it's free dad!" in-flight movie, and miss

"Tin Cup's" choosing to "go for it"
even though there's wind in his face
and water fronting the green;

or the armadillo meandering the panhandle
alone, backed by an accordion . . . :
"A little bit is better than nada."

Sam's too tall and hefty at 5'2"
and a-hundred-and twenty odd pounds
to sit on my lap for our return,

but since already it's Christmas day
in our projected time zone
he's in present-heaven and self-proficient

with his new CD's and video games.
He thrills to the first sight of land,
Brussels?, the lights scarce and intermittent

like survivors' last flares.
We're still over France, onetime Nazi strongholds
Vichy and Lyon.

The insomniacs have one advantage
over the sleepers: we can await the white
peaks, immense and various, like islands

above the turfy clouds that cover 360
sky-degrees and be there when black night gives way
to charcoal blue-gray to day-it-self-breaking.

Thousands have passed this way every day
since jet travel took over the skies,
but does that make it one bit

less miraculous?

VENICE: THE RETURN IN WINTER II

"Venice is sinking"—FERNAND BRAUDEL

I

Gliding along the Grand Canal before the ice
solidified, the buildings look like marble cliffs,
as if nature had quarried from human imagination
to blend diverse actions into one.

Gliding toward the invisible line
where lagoon opens onto open sea
we gaze at couples, arms around each other's
waists, setting out in the hazy dusk

toward Harry's Bar and the Gritti
to drink Negronis with famous ghosts.
The thresholds of palaces and churches
visible once more, shimmer.

Fifty people on the vaporetto.
Bundled in hats, scarves and gloves,
we're alone with a hundred restless
shifting eyes.

There's comfort in this collective
suffering which only one man
destroys, someone intent on being
debonair when it doesn't seem possible

as he stands on deck at the rail
in the wind, black hair slicked back, blue
blazer, pretending it was summer
and he was on his way to

a summer yacht party: cell phone,
spotless white slacks,
loafers, no socks, glancing
at his Rolex.

2

How do you know the Rolex *was real?*
Never once did you even hint
that his appearance might have been
like the wardrobe an actor puts on to play a part.
Have you ever heard the word gigolo?
Did you notice the binoculars he had slung over his shoulder?

It was the cell phone that grabbed my attention.
And black doesn't exactly contrast
with midnight blue.

But everyone in Italy has a cell phone.
No matter how negligible their income.

And many tourists carry high-powered binoculars.

You assumed that he wasn't a tourist,
but it is possible that you noticed
this fellow for reasons that still remain
unknown, and that he shouldered the binoculars
to scope out unaccompanied women
on the shore, or women with other women?

He looked like he was in his element.

I didn't say he wasn't Italian.

Thanks for the instructive interruption.
The path beckons for my return
but in the meantime we should both
consider the image forming
in the prism as we speak: assassin.

Stop! You're giving me goose pimples.
Who do you think he's there to kill?
Is the hit private, or public?

It's an all Italian special,
a great ancient family sending
out a reminder: "we're still here!

We didn't cry out against change.
We intermarried; moved elsewhere.
Scattered. In the diaspora.

Like others who were forced to trade
their countries for a condition:
exile. You never understood

the family fortress was a myth
and the old order long destroyed
before the wars exposed the rot."

Maybe it's to warn some neo-
retro movement they're being watched!

3

All values change in Venice. You fall in love for the first time not with a
woman but with a restaurant on Piazza Margherita.

Disgusted with our digs, we retreat
to a restaurant where we had delighted
in the *gnocchi con gorgonzola*
in that summer of the provocation,
and the owner's wife, who knows it is hell
to find a decent hotel room in Venice,

calls around while we get warm, and the chef's
American wife comes over to help
interpret. Once we're settled for one night
she joins us at our table. She loves living

in Venice but she gets lonely.
Every morning, she takes the train in from Mestre,
and walks the city. Knowing I need
an Ariadne, she agrees to gather me
at nine the next day and walk until we drop.
With fatigue caving in on my brain, I barter for another hour.

No, we didn't have to arrive during
the coldest spell winter has cast over
Italy in forty years, and no doubt
we should have brought warmer clothes, but life
has a certain strange trajectory of its own,
and the six-foot long and two-foot wide scarf
I purchased with Maria's help in bargaining
before we set out for the Giudecca on the Vaporetto,
proved vastly, fantastically malleable,
as I brought it over my mouth and head
when the cold wind off the water became
too much to bear. Maria claims to be
"flying" on the Thera-Flu she brought back
on her last trip to the states, I'm just grateful
for the magic scarf, which I vow never
to take off. Having disembarked, we walk
past shut-down storefronts and boarded-up houses

> For Sale,

since this day is too cold for the cafes
in a workers' quarter to remain
open, every door is bolted, except for the *tabacchi*
where the men who man the till endure
our presence only so long as we appear
to be about to purchase
                              something:
a smaller, lighter, made-to-scale
super-real Beretta for *ragazzo*,
a map, gum, or dusty elegant notebooks—
all to give our hands a chance to unfreeze.

Maria chats fluently with these men
but even she cannot delay
them brushing us aside.

The stores are so small (they can hardly hold
four customers plus one "salesperson")
that the men guarding the till say *grazie*
gruffly to get us to leave. Maria
tells me that Venice is a blue collar
town, many have never left, their futures
are determined at birth. Some gondoliers,
aware of obsolescence, live disgruntled lives,
resentful of their roles as tourist-servants,
and some of the many fishermen feel that way too.
But like lobstermen in Maine they also hate
to be away from their boats and the water for more than a day.
If she's right, and there's almost no
class mobility, then Venice is one
of the last great determinist
cities in Europe.

Adorable cats curl up on the Giudecca's thresholds; my guide warns
me not to pet them "because you don't know what they've eaten."
Enough said.

Downcast gondoliers.

The vaporettos are now manned by tall,
attractive, athletic women.

Then the Giudecca came to an end and we were up against San Gior-
gio Maggiori with no way to get there (stones treacherous)—and I
was suddenly in the mood to take refuge in a church.

*What about that place where they were performing Mass? The one there
merely to serve its parishioners.*

So while it's true that after hours walking against the bitter wind,
we were ready to return, I wish I hadn't let myself

think about   F O O D

4

Venice is disorientation.
Canal after canal dissolves,
and in the vertiginous whirl
(and the light beyond belief

beyond faith)

Salute collapses into Academia.

Riva into Fondamente,
Calle into Quay.

It's not the city that's exhausting
it's the language: lips and tongue
work to pronounce . . .
calamari scungilli
sinistra/destra

all one syllable words in English.

Venice at midnight: flares like the Greeks'
night encampment along Troy's shores.

Nothing
normalissimo about Venice.

Venice is—anti-simile. It isn't *like* any other place.

Now I meet them at the lovely pizzeria on the Zattere—
near the house where Ruskin plotted his raids
on buried porticos and vaults under canals,

but the child is a fussy eater, pizza won't do,
he must have pasta, plain,—sauce on the side—

and the woman must settle for eviscerated antipasto
and the man for grilled sole.

The child's noodles solamente
and alone and plain—NO SAUCE—
come wrapped, warped in menstrual marinara;
we send them back and repeat the order

this time miming
how to drain the noodles and place them on the plate,
senza marinara
and when his platter finally arrives
the second waiter, a genial young man,
can't keep from asking if he wouldn't
like "at least some butter . . . or olive oil . . ."

We exit gulping icy air.

6

Submerged like a diver in my watery sleep.

Voices
carry across the water.

A man to a woman in an outboard on a lagoon:
"There's only one way to treat passion.
Tempt it to destruction."

7

Code Name: "Maria's Restaurant"

"Ah, but have you tried the Sardinian wine?"

Only because I have not yet begun
    to imbibe this sacred source
can I summon the strength to say we'll stay
    with the Chianti 1990 or Riserva '93.

The spirited youths at the long table
    don't hesitate over paying another
20,000 for the more exotic Sardinian
    and devour platters of lemons.

Venice seduces. Why try to evoke
    how the spell's cast? Or how the city
breaks down your resistance?
    Bottles bottles bottles,

the apertifs and digestifs made from
    innumerable herbs.
The icy wind which transforms
    an after dinner walk

into an expedition in the dark
    through unknown alleys,
and over echoing canals, onto
    the Zattere under

Orion's' blaze just as the hunter lets go
    of the quivering bow
and the arrow wriggles across
    the pitch-blackness like a comet,

as clear as Carnevale lights.
        But this is not a night
to stand outside staring at the sky
        for too long and now,

with toes and fingers frozen I want
        the quickest route
to a crackling fire, and black coffee
        laced with grappa.

8

Remember, not all of Venice is fake. The essence of Venice is inven-
tion, even if every stone is where it is for a reason. The islands and the
canals were there before Marco Polo, the India Cafe, Cinemascope,
Ruskin and Turner. The Romans called the tribes that lived in Venice
the Veniti. The tribes stretched from Trieste to the mouth of the Po.
The early settlers confronted a world of mud and marshes stirred by
the tides. Deserted shorelines in the dark. Mantua could have
remained a marshland were it not for the Jews' architectural ingenu-
ity.

The Veniti were also there before
the inscrutable woman, fine cheekbones,
only an inch or so of whitened skin
shining between sunglasses and bright
orange down hat with ear flaps immersed in
the German journal *Mercure*, before the raft
where you wait to catch the vaporetto
began to bob rhythmically, and millions of
bizarrely curious people began to pour
throughout the maze, this labyrinth, this

Venice,
        where we walk through sightless alleys barely
wider than my shoulders, and exit on
other canals where long branches, unpruned
perhaps for centuries, reach out from wild
gardens which sprawl below dilapidated palazzos

spared restoration . . . , and a creature,
somewhere between a duck and a pigeon,
forages in the frigid canal. . . .

When you think of the numerous, not to say numberless,
artists and writers, who fled to Italy —I'm surprised
that you would not search for less trammeled locations,
like Lisbon, or Barcelona, but not . . .

Every trip has been so harried in its own peculiar way, that I left each
time feeling fascinated but unsatisfied, as if I had just touched the sur-
face. The total number of days spent in Italy in three separate visits
before this return in winter amount to no more than a month and a
half. All in early summer, when the city, while not being sacked, is
still under siege.

You can spend half a day in Rome or Venice finding the church with the
paintings that you want to see. And on each excursion detours distract you
from your ostensible purpose.

There is a suffering that exists and can't be eradicated; blame can't be
placed on one thing or another.

I saw more of Venice in a day on a tour than you've yet shown me.
Scarcely a monument shows up in your pages. Yours is a Venice without a
Doge's Palace, Veronese's Rape of Europa, *the crystal mystery, the jeweled*
sea, coral, amethyst.

I tried to elide that which has already been documented, too often
described.

But if Hofmanstall, Ruskin, Stokes and Pound, within the last hundred
years, didn't hesitate to call the city crystalline . . .

The azure air and the water blend
together and are then transformed into a
matter that matters; substances
like water, air, and stone
intermingle.

They praised the city's early visionary builders justly but overdid the
"incomparable" transient beauty bit?

Those two gigantic gilded globes
in the Doge's apartment
signify an arrogance . . .

an ambition . . . —far beyond what's implied
by the maps of the world on the walls
in numerous paintings you don't need me to name—

an illusion, that if you possess
the biggest and best
representations of the known
world it's almost
like running it.

What? The world?

Yes, considering that by the late 1500s the dukes were far
from alone in estimating that Venice had become
the true center.

And these late Venetian dukes before the fall,
whose fine taste in art and architecture is still
everywhere in evidence, far from being at all
like the brutal power-mongers who bulldozed
history before and after, were relatively
benevolent despots, and kept some perspective
with regard to this

LARGER PICTURE

(though in their obsessing with maps resemble
today's fanatics
who like to surf the Internet to find out
everything about everything past and present
without leaving their rooms).

I thought you said moons.

Grandeur exhausts me.

Venice too.

Why not click into the interiors or blow up details you can't even see when you're there?

I can hardly . . .

9

Jet lag and the aggravation of a foghorn-like sound.

We sit up late into the night
in our room at the American Hotel,
she in her nightgown with her legs
tucked under her
                                        sipping Jack Daniels,
sobbing, barebreast
face wet against my neck—

the canal menacing on the unlit
Fondamente.

I made mental preparations for being lost.
I like being adrift.
And to move freely in the mist.

But, I want to see my lover's face,
her breasts ears eyes and turfy mound
and glance down—from time
to time—as her thighs part
more and more and more.

I want to look at the woman I'm touching—

and since you insist—I will
CONFESS,
that in the act in the pitch
blackness
she is more herself
than she is she,
or could be . . .

as we swell more deeply
and lose ourselves in
sex itself, the sex
of sex, selfless in the loss;

another woman now:
at that instant almost any other woman.

10

When we quarrel, my wife and I,
while traveling, it's usually about how
to spend this costly, invaluable time.

The triangle: two parents (male and female)
and one child (male or female), is its own hell.
In theory, all three could go their own way
but when there's a child involved
parents often straddle
their positions and decisions,

never more than when their offspring
is too young to be on his own.

Or I might not want to go somewhere I've already been,
but neither she nor I want him setting out
into the Venetian maze alone,

and we're equally afraid of missing out
on the splendors that turn up unexpectedly
all the time in Venice,

or the child's face lighting up with
delight or awe.

But at dusk the night before we asked Sam if we could run over to the nearby Peggy Guggenheim museum which stayed open until 7 while he took a nap ("I don't take naps!") or had a Sprite at the bar in the lobby, and charged it to the room.

(The latter stratagem had worked before when we were in deep need of a half an hour alone in our room in Milan. In Kanab, Utah, we went even further. While Sam took refuge in the air-conditioned room when it was 119° outside, we said we'd "be back in ten minutes" while we "cased the joint," then asked the first (friendly-looking) maid we saw if could borrow a room she hadn't finished making up and she turned the key in the lock and I slipped her a twenty and took full advantage of the unused bed and returned, somewhat breathless, to tell Sam that the pool stayed open until 11.)

"OK. But can I just go down the block and get some chocolate? I know my way. I won't get lost." What could happen? We could almost see the street across the bridge from our room. "Sure."

Since the museum staff was fidgeting at this awkward hour, though too well mannered to pressure us overtly, we chose to look only at the Giacometti's, which provided an oblique mirror to our mood. Figures in motion. Man as a walking animal. Figures falling away from each other, any center, just as his models decomposed each time they returned for another sitting, rational people who wanted Alberto to stop before he further insulted their narcissism and "ruined what was clearly finished" to everyone except the painter. I thought of his drawings of figures walking off the page, napkin, or tablecloth and how their movement reminded me now of Venice itself, where people pass continually over quays and bridges while the waves ripple and plash under their footsteps. Repetition is undone in Venice.

And was he home when you returned?

His body was there. But just as we had meditated on Giacometti, he had meditated on the super-realistic Beretta in the window of an upscale tabacchi and insisted I see it before he had dinner or he wouldn't come. Though plastic, the toy gun, or was it a weapon?, came with pellets, and cost many times more than the one I had seen on the Giudecca. Sam was right, it looked just like a real Beretta, an imitation that verged on the authentic. I might have thought it was a gun if I hadn't picked it up: only its weight, or lack of it, is what gave it away. "Do you like it Dad?" "I do, but it's expensive, and you know how your mother feels about guns." "But that's why I asked you to look at it."

Add this conversation to what I said earlier about marriage. My generation grew up playing with toy guns, no one I know came to harm. Sam was born into such a violent world that most of the parents I know have outlawed guns and the children have for the most part adjusted: they don't want to provoke lunatics in public any more than we do. If price wasn't an issue I probably would have sprung for the gun and trusted Sam to use it only in the house. But "probably" wasn't a strong enough reason to provoke my wife, so I placed it back in its box.

"Aw' come on Dad, it's the same gun James Bond uses."
"It is a swell gun but it looks so real I'd be afraid to have it in my bag at the airport."
"But it's only plastic! And it's the gun Bond substitutes for the one 'M' gives him in *Dr. No.*"
"But it has metal parts."
"Come on Dad, you guys never get me anything I want."
"What about the CD's and games . . ."
"Those were Christmas presents!"
I pretend not to hear that rejoinder.
"And I don't want you flashing a gun that looks so real some crazy person might shoot at you. You're a tall boy, what if a cop saw you flashing it under a streetlight at night and yelled 'halt!' and 'put up your hands' and you started to tell the cop you were just a kid and it was just a toy by which time . . ."
Now I hated myself for perhaps overdoing the scare tactics so he wouldn't take out his disappointment on me.
"Besides, you could hurt someone with those pellets."

"You had a B-B gun when you were eleven!"
"And I lived in a small town with a backyard
where I could fire at bottles and cans and not fear
hitting anything but trees if I missed."

Madelaine was adamant about the Doge's Palace. Sam railed. I went
along in a sulk to prove I was right how miserable an experience it
would be on a day like this. They got on my wrong side by rushing up
the steps with a group of Japanese tourists. Ceaselessly searching I
happened on all the rooms I mentioned but no wife, no son. Anxious,
and also weary of being abandoned by them in public places I head
for the rest room, where brackish water pours under the greenish
wooden gates. They're standing in line with people from Europe,
Asia, the Netherlands, and elsewhere. The tense silence is violently
interrupted when a small, dark-haired, Italian boy, rustles a cello-
phane bag each time he reaches into THE NORMALISSIMO CHIPS. A
man who I hope is his father exits the toilet while zipping his fly: the
two crunch and crackle with an unreal fervor.

II

But would there have been a way to prepare for Venice this winter
when everything you've seen . . . fog fog fog in the dark wind
blows off the canal and crawls insidiously under your clothes
and you think it will pass and you'll be back at your hotel

momentarily but time stretches out, as they say it does in hell.

Now it's tomorrow the sun's gone
the Academia bridge is a fine place to stand at dusk,
the canal drifts
far
in two directions before it
carries away away . . .

my mood lifts in the red-gray haze
to strains of Monteverdi in the small cafe.

And at the rattling of cups.

It pains me to think of leaving
Venice without another glimpse
of Carpaccio's ships, sails full,
deck crowded with Venetians

and Orientals from all classes;
courtesans, pirates, astronomers, merchants,
with bell towers woven into the background,
for who can say when we will return?—

12

At the Fiore on our last night, we are seated beside a long-haired man, disheveled, tattered coat, gloves, who lingers over wine and hand-rolled cigarettes long after the waitress has removed the remains of his fowl. They're out of all the wines that interest me, I refuse Cabernet Sauvignon and relate how the northern Californian coast is gripped by snow, and the waiter says no, these are Venetian wines, no problem, and the man alone at the next table holds up his bottle of Malcontenta and nods and I nod to the waiter that we'll have what he has, dark, ripe, and rich, like a potion. After we down our first glass he orders a second bottle, an act I find incomprehensible for a man alone. Cognac and cafe macchiato would make more sense . . . how much wine can one man alone, *l'uomo solo*, imbibe with . . . pleasure?

13

New Year's Eve day. Mestre
desolate in the gray air.
Murano in mist and smoke.

Too few vaporettos to accommodate
the crowds, unsteady bodies on
unsteady planks—

"The last time it snowed in Padua, Florence, or Rome
was twelve years ago."

"But was it horizontal snow?"

No one wishing they were here this winter.

Except the tireless equilibrist from Geneva,
boyish charm, good cheer, unruffled hair,
who insists on small talk in the lobby
while Sam and I thaw out,
hot chocolate, grappa, a fire in the grate,
sinister whine off the windy canal,
American films dubbed into Italian . . .

"Think of it," he thinks to say,
"one New Year's Day eve
the weather was the same
in Venice and San Francisco."

"But not in Melbourne."

"No, in Melbourne it's summer."

Death Becomes Her takes on another dimension
in the foreign tongue in Venice,
reflecting the beauty and sadness of an actress' dilemma
when no wants to cast her as a romantic lead
after she's forty-something.

Is there a forward age moving toward us
when women will no longer be positioned
in terms of age?

Why stereotype people according to sex

when ALL earthlings are so different?

For more reasons than are dreamt of in Freud's biology.

14

Only the slits of my eyes are visible
between my hatbrim and my scarf.
Plunging headlong into arctic gusts—
I cross Calle Lion to reach

Scuola di San Giorgio degli Schiavone,
where Carpaccio's St Jerome
is rumored to have become St Augustine.
I try the door. It is bolted shut.

It's hard to stand still with frigid air
coming in off the water.
In a futile lifelong quest for equanimity
I force myself to acknowledge I've been there

twice before and that it's the city itself
I've returned to explore.
Easy to say, but hard, hard
to memorize when you're mesmerized.

The ingenious patrons and architects of Venice
and environs, the Malatestas and the Palladios,
like their near contemporaries
from DaVinci to Machiavelli

will, as if immunized by Zeno's paradox,
remain forever ahead of the belated
laborers doomed to reconstructing
Venice at its height.

15

We depart on a gray morning. Pigeons wheeling like desperadoes over
the dome of Santa Maria della Salute. Across the canal, the moorings
are painted like barber poles. A worker pushes a rusted wheelbarrow
down the Fondamenta. An ambulance passes under the Academia

bridge, as if to demonstrate the Doppler Effect for a group of schoolchildren. The brick facades on Calle Pasina are badly in need of work. A gondolier presses hard on his oar to bear his six Japanese passengers between three motorboats

Polizia Lagunaire

Polizia Municipale

and one civilian boat heaped with square white bags. Having walked down hundreds of alleys in less than seven days, I am more lost than ever.

The maze grows and no one who lives here appears to know a better way.

16

Venice is a mystery beyond solution.

But it's held together by geometry.

There are reasons mathematical, which include factoring in the dimension of time, as to why the pattern cannot be detected.

Maybe. But while everyone I know remembers the moment in elementary school when, during history, the teacher pulled the map down over the blackboard and pointed to the point about Italy that

doesn't bear repeating,

and only after being lost so often in the devious passageways and alleys where every stone commands attention, and I reached a place where I could visualize the city as a whole, did I realize that Venice, too, is shaped like a boot.

You suffer nobly, but never learn anything. Maps are like clouds. And clouds are like whales or riderless horses. Or God's furrowed brow.

There's no design?

I didn't say that! And I like your idea that one ingenious architect picked up where the other left off and went on, in secret, in silence, keeping the pattern alive while satisfying his commissioner. But how is that different from the Talmud's tradition of commentaries?

Language is more malleable than stone.

Like your son you're often frighteningly right in point and devious in the way you elide the answer. The forest of symbols is far more deceptive than the dark wood.

There is no such thing as complete understanding.

In Italy all weather collects under one sky.
Tonight, on New Year's Eve, from rooftops
all over Rome, there will be
a rumble from behind
rancorous clouds
as fireworks light up the seven hills,
like a series of small battles.

IN YOUR OWN TIME

Stratton, snow-covered, radiant in winter light;
but the branches creaking at the limit
of how much ice and snow they can uphold.
If a god remains, it's weather.

Time hasn't changed resistance to change.
Wind rocks your car, forces a poplar grove to its knees.
Still you won't act on what your eyes have seen
without switching on the Weather Channel.

Power lines down. Shake hands with the real.
Too late to have a cord delivered. And—no cable!
Take heed to wield a whetted axe-blade.
But before you set out to reclaim your inner

hunter-gatherer, open the flues, get every fireplace
roaring, then see what condition the woodstove's in.
Ice-cold, ashes piled high inside, but no rust—
despite not having tasted a slow burning log

since the day you put in central heating.
Splitting logs in the sub-zero air you sweat,
find a rhythm, suddenly can' t . . . see.
Must be dark. Take a step

toward home; slide: almost slip.
Flashlights, familiar voices: "stay where you are!"
Slick underfoot, this frozen world.
A woman and a child take hold of your arms.

"All this happened since I left?"
"It was zero. Now it's twenty below."
Now is the time to break out the family
crystal and that four year old Sabine wine

you've hoarded: for no sooner have the winds
stopped howling in unthinkable depths
than waves too high for any half-sane
surfer-hero to even think about riding,

crash rock-cliff, claw birch and pine.
Reprieves? There are no reprieves.
Bless being here to breathe the living air.
Live your youth, life's gift.

Hang with your friends, chances are
you'll never lay eyes on most of them again
after senior year recedes in the eternal past tense.
Then there's the girl. The one you had a crush on.

The one riding in the corral the day you visited the school.
The one you stopped to watch every day just before noon,
between history and lunch, train her horse
to stop and start and turn so quick

you'd miss it if you blinked.
Day students and boarders rarely mingled.
Her candor won you over.
"Look at those two horses fucking,"

she remarked as a stallion mounted
a mare. From then we shared a free
exchange of glances. She often smiled.
Dying to ask her out I was sure there had to be

a better time and place. Two years went by,
and our speech was limited to these
cursory "hi"s and my semi-muttering her name
when, before the lunch bell rang,

she and her horse became one as they cleared
the fence, took the trail to the barn at full
gallop, and vanished in the unvanquished
dust. Like the years.

In the middle of my life's way
I'm driving in the desert, when a
turn-off for Phoenix brings with it her image.
I swerve toward the detour but stop

to check the phone book. Not a trace.
The Sonoran desert was her home.
But she's probably listed under another
last name—even if divorced from some guy

who'd been unworthy of her.
Second chances spawn in chance's domain.
But in cases where a mortal holds back and looks
when they ought to have acted the gods are

reluctant to repeat an offer. What use
if you've failed to grasp that time is irrecoverable?
So, school yourself in idleness
now, while time still unrolls seamlessly

as space. Learn through vigilance not to let that mask of
look how cool I am become your face,
so that you don't back away from asking
this girl you "don't really know" to the prom,

or that you fail to stroll
the undulating knolls and piazzas
where you might encounter,
(in the low whispers as night comes on)

a flirtatious glance, a secretive touch,
the shy girl obscured in the dark, far corner,
her laughter's mysterious sign once you slip
the token from her finger, and take her hand.

(*after Horace, Odes, Book I, 9*)

Notes

The italicized voice is often, but not always, that of the "rider" from *Rider*.

"Against Odds Against," "The Desert of Empire," and "In Your Own Time" are part of a series of Horatian Palimpsests that began with "Role Play" in *The Millennium Hotel*. I attempt to transpose an American context onto Horace's Roman world, and replace or amplify some of his mythic references with contemporary ones: the hecatombs of bulls and the gloomy stream are recast as figures from the epic Western *Red River*, his depiction of Roman decadence, promiscuous women and philandering men, is set in a sex club in our nation's capital city; and Mount Soracte becomes Stratton Mountain in Vermont—and sometimes his counsel inspires digressions that become poems within the poem.

The lines that the history teacher murmurs in "Across a Crowded Room" are adapted from Goethe's "Gesang der Geiser uber den Wassern" (1779).

In the winter of 1996 I was rereading René Char and, frustrated by being limited essentially to what editors had chosen to include in several American "Selected Poems," when a friend told me she was going to Paris, I asked if she would purchase his complete works in the Pleiade for me if possible. She did, and I began reading poems that as far as I know had never been published in English translations. I was drawn to "Jeanne Qu'on Brula Verte," (a prose poem in the original French) because it was different from the kind of aphoristic poem Char is best known for here, and because it was elusive in other ways. It was while I began to adapt Char's poem that I began to think again about LePage's painting.

Jean Seberg found her way into "Joan and Jean" when I read a sentence in a review of Mark Rappaport's fictionalized documentary *From the Journals of Jean Seberg* in the New York Times which mentioned that the actress was literally burned during the pyre scene in *Saint Joan*. I wanted to keep the historical Joan in the foreground of the poem, but was propelled to write the second postscript when I happened on Carlos Fuentes's fascinating and surprising "novel" about his thinly disguised affair with Jean Seberg, *Diana:*

The Goddess of the Hunt (HarperPerennial, 1996). She was becoming more and more intriguing, and ambiguous. Here is her account of the pyre scene: "the director [Otto Preminger] didn't understand that [Joan was a revolutionary] . . . The idiot thought Joan was a saint because she suffered, not because she enjoyed being intolerable for everyone. The director tied me to the stake, he ordered the fire lit, and he didn't even film the scene. He watched how the flames came closer . . . to see me terrified so he could make me into his Saint Joan. He should have let me be burned up then and there, the son of a bitch. The crew saved me when the flames were touching my robe. The director was happy. I had suffered: I was a saint. He didn't let me be a rebel. We both failed" (p. 75). *From the Journals of Jean Seberg*, with its seamless weaving of fact and fiction, further thickened the broth. I would like to thank Karen Bender, Mary Beth Hurt, and Mark Rappaport for their help with this poetic sequence.

The lines beginning with "It doesn't drift like bait any more, this city," are derived from Rainer Maria Rilke's poem "Spatherbst in Venedig" (from the book *Der neuen Gedichte anderer Teil*, 1908). Boris Pasternak formed his image of the poet from fleeting glimpses of Rilke—who was a friend of his father Leonid—and began his autobiography *Safe Conduct* with an image of Rilke boarding a train.

Pasternak, after abandoning his desire to become a composer, went to Marburg, Germany, to study with the reknowned philosopher Hermann Cohen. Part of my long-time fascination with this obscure, very early poem of Pasternak's was his ambition "to contain the city of Venice" in terms that are usually reserved for architecture.